FRAGMENTS OF WASTED DEVOTION

FRAGMENTS OF WASTED DEVOTION

MIA ARIAS TSANG

ILLUSTRATED BY LEVI WELLS

QUILTED PRESS

info@quiltedpress.com
quiltedpress.com

This book depicts actual events in the author's life as truthfully as recollection permits. All persons within are actual individuals; there are no composite characters. Dialogue has been reconstructed from memory. The author in no way represents any company, corporation, or band mentioned in this book.

Text copyright © 2025 by Mia Arias Tsang.
Art copyright © 2025 by Levi Wells.

No part of this book may be reproduced, or stored in a retrieval system, or transmitted in any form or by any means, electronic, mechanical, photocopying, recording, or otherwise, without express written permission of the author, except for the use of brief quotation in a book review or critical / academic essay.

Many of these pieces were previously published elsewhere or contain short quotes from other works. See "Attributions" section at the end of this book for more info.

Cover design: Rachel Ake
Interior design: Paul Tsang

ISBN (paperback): 979-8-9896691-5-8

CONTENTS

CAMBRIDGE	1
TEMPERATURE CHECK	2
SUMMER 2019	7
FIRST YEAR	10
RAIN	28
I WANT TO BE ON THE GOLDEN STATE WARRIORS DANCE TEAM	33
MELATONIN DREAMS	34
ANYWHERE WITH YOU COULD BE NEW YORK	40
LONGING DISTANCE	42
CRAVE	50
THE WOMAN WHO KNOWS	56
VENICE	58
UNIDENTIFIED AERIAL PHENOMENON OVER MANHATTAN AVENUE	62
LETTER TO AN OLD ARCHITECT	66
YOU SAID EVERY TIME YOU HIT YOUR VAPE YOU THINK OF ME	88
THE CONSEQUENCES OF TRUTH	90
HARDLINE	102
AOTY	104
PRELUDE TO A PROMISE I KNEW I WOULD BREAK	116
ANATOMY OF BREAKUP SEX	120

For you

I want to tell you this story without having to be in it:
—Richard Siken, "The Torn-Up Road"

I'm sick of the ending.
—Yumi Zouma, "KPR"

CAMBRIDGE

My heart was too young to be so settled, but I laid it down on your chest anyway. I refused to be the one to separate – not until I knew we wouldn't dissolve after. Your world never ends how you think it will.

In my childhood bedroom there are three white walls and one bright blue. You can write on that one. It's designed for it. But now it's my headboard and the chalk dust would choke my pillow, so I don't. I don't do a lot of things. Listen to signs, for one. I would write them down if I were braver. A list of everything I refused to understand. Your opacity. Your cigarettes. Your woman, flowers blooming across her skin. All hang like icicles from the ceiling, melting loose with my wanting to fall and slit my throat in the night.

In your dorm room there were four blue walls. There were no rules, so you wrote on one in black spray paint. You were crossed. You barely remembered it. At least that's what you told me, laughing, as I ran my finger across the words and wondered if they'd come off on me. That night you didn't hold me as we slept beneath Keith Haring: *Ignorance = fear. Silence = death.*

TEMPERATURE CHECK

It's ninety degrees in July and I'm sweating through blue sheets that aren't ruined yet. I'm naked and texting a boy who asks me why I'm still awake. *i have trouble sleeping in the heat*, I say. *aw :(i'm sorry*, he says. *i'm not bc it keeps me awake to talk to you*, I say. I don't mean this. I don't mean any of it. It's summer in Connecticut so I don't have to tell him the truth when the earth will do it for him. The atmosphere will sweat us out. I can lie because the world has never been as green as it is right now. I can lie because I tell myself once he finally baptizes me on cotton and springs I will be fixed. I won't have to lie anymore. But his hands are shy and I can't wait that long. At least, that's what I say when I give up on him.

It's seventy degrees in September and I'm sitting on your couch. I've reached my personal best. I've never met her before tonight but you bring her out. You make me. In the hands-to-clay way. In the build-me-up-from-dust-and-sweat-into-something-you-can-break way. You kill me kiss me make me *feel*. I was never broken.

It's fifty degrees in March and I'm standing on sand four feet away from the boy who once asked me why I was still awake. I'm freezing in my turtleneck and overalls but would rather die than admit it. He confessed he is afraid of me, so I feel safe. I know the words for what I am now and that's why I'm here with him against my better judgment. I want to set him free but there's never a good time, he's looking at me that way again and I just know he'll never hear me. *You look like you're going to control a lot of people someday,* he says. *I don't think so,* I say. *Okay,* he says and I hate the way he says it, like he doesn't believe me. Like he knows me better than I know myself.

It's forty degrees in October and I'm sitting on your couch again. You're in boxers and a turtleneck and a tiny black beanie and you're turning on the AC. *What are you doing?* I ask. You turn and say *I'm hot, aren't you?* And I'm in a literal tank top in *October* so I say *It's October, maybe it's because you're still wearing that beanie.*

You say *Shut up* and chuckle and are you blushing? Are you going soft on me? *I can't sleep unless the room is freezing,* you say, and I laugh at you. I lie. I say *You're ridiculous* I say *I don't understand* even though you can read my mind so you can see sweat drying on my blue sheets and you know what I would give to shiver. I just don't want you to know me so easily but of course you can see through glass, there isn't much to know here, I am not a complicated person and I just love you.

It's thirty degrees in a long-forgotten February and my blue sheets are ruined. Theory would call it violence but theory calls everything violence and that's why I can't read it. You know how it is. Boy meets girl neither were drinking the lights were on all that fucking nonsense. Just stupid. Just noise. *I feel used*, he says and that's rich isn't it? I wouldn't be a vessel for his body but he still hollowed me out. His long fingers still pressed their lines into my skin. He still got mad. He deserves my pleasure more than I do. And he said sorry. He said sorry, so I force myself to drink the kool-aid but it turns to vodka halfway down and I won't get back the days after, not a single one.

No, I say when you ask if you can —————, just to see what happens. To let my tongue taste the word, just once. You say *Okay* and kiss my thigh. You don't say anything else.

Fuck, I say because you're touching me and my vision goes white and I'm not sure what to do with all this pleasure except ruin it. You stare my breaking in the eye and decide no more. *Are you okay?* you ask and I can only look at you and breathe.

Stop, I say, just to see what you'll do.

You do.

SUMMER 2019

The day I realized you didn't love me, I walked four miles and pushed you out with every step. In Connecticut June we're just getting to the heat, so I didn't start to sweat until I was almost home. You would know how I get lost sometimes if you paid attention. Did you know in East Rock there's a house with a giant American flag on the corner of a street called "Eagle?" If only we could laugh at the heavy-handedness, but you'll just think I'm trying to impress you. I'll have to add this to the list of things I'm too proud to tell you anymore.

The day I realized you didn't love me, I found a deck of cards in the grass on the side of the road, so warped by nature and burn that the ink bled through from the backs and turned them into fifty-one midnight skies. I tried to make it mean something that the only legible card was the six of spades – breaking dirt, shallow graves – but I'm not a poet like you. Sometimes things don't mean. Sometimes things just are.

The day I realized you didn't love me, I listened to *Pure Heroine* all the way through for the first time since the last time I broke my own heart. What's different is you care. What's the same is I let so much slide. Messy kisses dropped on my forehead at your doorstep. Schemes to attend the same MFA program after graduation. Declarations of love after five drinks. A long line of boys who think they're men, letting you down over and over again. Your heart is a muscle the size of the *better world* you're striving to build. I was doomed to love an aspiring revolutionary. You never hesitate to chastise my nihilism. You're the only one who can get away with talking to me the way you do.

The day I realized you didn't love me, I deveined kale that had gone yellow in the crisper drawer of this kitchen that has only barely been mine and thought about how I keep failing. When I was sixteen, my mother once asked me how I could know I was gay when I couldn't even wash the dishes. How can I hold you in my heart when I can't eat my groceries before they rot? I could never read you when you were here in this city with me, but now that you're gone it crystallizes. *Kiss me,* you have been saying *I'm out of my mind* you have been saying *I cannot be brave* you have been saying *you need to cross this line for me* you have been saying *we both know how this ends.*

FIRST YEAR *You'd have to stop the world just to stop the feeling.*
—Chappell Roan, "Good Luck, Babe!"

"Nonconsensual relentless nostalgia"? Just say you miss me. Just pick up your fucking phone and tell me you miss me. Tell me you're sorry. Tell me it was because we didn't have sex and you never liked me, and your heart never raced the way you felt mine did.

Tell me about your new boyfriend. How he kisses better and that's not fair because it was my first time and you knew that. How he fucks you and that's not fair because it would have been my first time and you knew that. How he doesn't love you and that's not fair because I did, and you knew that.

I don't want to hear you tell me, again, how *important* I am. How *incredible* I am. If I were really all those *i*'s you wouldn't have replaced me so quickly. I don't want your platitudes. I want you to tell me about the imbalance you felt between us. Tell me about my devotion and the power it gave you. Tell me about the moment you thought of what you might feel later and how it scared you.

And then tell me the truth.

*

It is early February and I am sitting in the library trying

to read a Han Kang book about female starvation. Priya is beside me, typing away on her tiny, shiny, pink MacBook Air. She asks me to read her longform poem, or lyric, or whatever it's called, and then asks for notes. It is composed of phrases and words I couldn't even hope to link together myself. It is brilliant and beautiful and perfect, and she wants notes. Criticism.

I'm not the right person to be asking for this, I say.

That's not true, she says.

I squint into the blue twilight outside the window. The air is fuzzy. It takes a minute to tell if it's snowflakes or spots in my own vision. I look up at the street lamp. It's snow. I can see the flakes glow gold against the light.

Will I ever be a writer? Am I a writer if I cannot write like Priya, like Monique?

I stare down at the book in my lap with a new distaste. What good has it done, all these years spent reading all these words, if what I write does not move?

*

A letter to your new best friend:

I'm sorry I unfollowed you on Instagram, and Twitter, and Facebook. It's not personal. I just couldn't bear to see your body filling the outline I left behind.

*

It is mid-September and I am in my common room on the phone, talking to Michael. You are still with Simon. It is seven and you are having sex or whatever it is two people in love do when the sun sets. I tell him about this. He does not hear the tears on the edge of my voice.

You deserve more than waiting, he says.

When we hang up, I lie on my back on the couch. And because he told me not to, I don't wait. I just happen to be doing nothing when you text me.

*

It is mid-December. It's been a week since I have seen your face. I wake up with my sheets drenched in sweat. It's been a week since I have heard your voice. I open Twitter. It's been a week since you have bruised my heart. You've started seeing a new boy.

Now it's been thirty seconds.

Have you always been this cruel, or did I awaken it in you?

If you wanted to have sex, you could have just asked me.

*

Listen, I'm not a writer. I have tried my hardest to sound like what I think a writer sounds like, but the fact of the matter is, I can't. So I'm not.

My writing isn't Brian's writing, writing that says *fuck that*, aiming for Kerouac, pretentious violent metaphors for what he thinks life is. My writing isn't Monique's writing, writing that says *burn it down*, every word an assertion of power in a world that seeks to rip it from their hands. My writing isn't Priya's writing, writing that says *green*, flowing flourishing diasporic sentences that move like liquid, like consciousness, like what I've been told good writing is. My writing isn't your writing, writing that says *I am*, declaring itself pure and distilled, without embellishment or apology.

I am overwhelmed with directions to take, boxes to check, advice to follow. Strip down the detail and specificity. Let your audience read between the lines, they say. Baffle them with metaphor. Insinuate, show-don't-tell. Capture the feeling and never define it. But I tell, because I am honest. I tell, because I am a storyteller. I tell stories. There's no such thing as a storyshower.

Okay, fine, putting that Lykke Li song on your playlist was a bit much.

*

It is early December and I am lying in your bed. It is two in the morning and only the second time I have ever been in your room. Beside me you murmur, shift, twist your legs with mine.

It's too hot. I roll onto my back and run my fingers through the mesh of your Ikea curtains in the blue light, sliding in and out of consciousness. I need air.

I slip out from beneath the blankets, taking care not to wake you. The hallway outside your room is dark and cool. I shiver. No windows here, only shadows. It is deathly quiet. I can't hear the wind in the trees or the sirens in the city or even your roommates, and I wonder for a moment if we are the only two people left in the world.

In the bathroom I pee, then stand in front of the sink looking at myself in the mirror. I am wearing your shirt, and my hair is still curly. I can feel the ghost of your lips against mine. I take a picture with my phone. This is something I think I want to remember.

I return to your room. For a moment I stand by your desk, taking in the shape of you. I don't want to break your peace by squeezing back into your twin XL just yet, but I also don't want to take the chance that you'll wake and see me watching you. Why I'm afraid of this, I'm not sure. I think I shouldn't be. I think maybe this is a sign. I leave my phone on your desk and ease myself as carefully as possible back under the sheets. It's no use. You feel the sudden dip of the mattress and turn to me. There's confusion in your squinting eyes. You didn't even know I was gone.

Hey, you say, and the affection in your voice cracks me open. You aren't mad that I've disturbed you. In fact, you are smiling huge. It is the first time I have seen you so open.

Sorry, I whisper. But you are already turning away from me.

*

It is late September and you are reeling. Simon has left you and you are manic. I watch you unravel across the table in front of me. You can barely form coherent words, let alone sentences. You are grinning, even on the verge of tears. I am not afraid. I think I should be.

He said he's 'afraid he's going to fall in love with me,' you say, with air quotes. *Isn't that just such bullshit?*

Isn't it?

In the moment, I laugh. You think it's because I find it as ridiculous as you do. But I actually think I understand him. He was a fool to let you go, but he was smart enough to save himself from you.

*

I still listen to the playlist sometimes — *dear mia // here are songs for grey fall days* — because damn it all to hell, you have good taste in music.

Why haven't you deleted it?

*

It is early November and I am riding the SafeRide shuttle back to my dorm from Priya's. It is 10pm and I have just told her all about you. I managed to hide it for most of the semester, but over *Scandal* and popcorn the emotion spews out of me. She thinks I ought to tell you how I feel but I am afraid that what actually ends up happening will eventually end up happening.

The SafeRide is empty and the light inside is all red. I take a picture of the first-aid kit that says *BODY FLUIDS* on it because the light makes it look like an emergency. I wish you were here so that I could take a picture of you instead to see what your face would look like underneath. When I get back to my dorm I feel lighter than I have in weeks.

I take off my clothes and pour myself a full cap of ZzzQuil. I need to medicate myself to sleep without dreaming of you.

*

You told me once that I am a good writer. You also told me once that you had feelings for me. I have no choice but to disregard it all.

*

If you want to get your first kiss, here's what you have to do.

It is late September and we are walking back to my dorm from Popeyes, where I just spent the past twenty minutes trying not to throw up. It is a Friday night and I have had five shots and apparently not enough water. I am complaining to you about how despite my best efforts, I cannot seem to get anyone to like me enough to kiss me. I am, of course, talking about you. But you don't know this, and you've taken it upon yourself to help me. At least, I think this is what this is.

You then proceed to list a few steps for me to follow. *Go out with someone you like, get drunk, dance with them all night, and flirt a little bit. Then, at the end of the night, you kiss them.*

We stop in front of my dorm. *Yeah, well.* I look at you. *I don't know.*

I wonder if you realize you just recited in order everything you and I did together tonight. I briefly consider asking. But then I remember that it has only been days since Simon ended things. Of course you want me to kiss you. You are lonely, and I am convenient.

So instead I hug you and say goodnight, and try to be content with your arms around my waist.

*

Capitalize my name when you're talking to me. This may come as a surprise to you, but I'm a person, not an object.

It is still early December and I am sitting on the edge of your bed, fully dressed. Your shirt is folded beside me. You are showering, so I look around at the photographs of your family you took on 35mm and the drawings of hands you did in ink and the letter your little sister had written to you on a typewriter as I wait for you. Sitting there, seeing all of this, I realize I have only just begun to scratch the surface of you. There is so much left for me to learn. My heart feels fuller than I ever imagined it could feel.

You come back in with wet hair and new clothes. Your smile is tight. I suggest breakfast. You say you have a lot of work to do. You are tense. You don't kiss me. You put your arms around me, and then I leave.

I try not to think about how you look at me differently in the daylight.

*

It is mid-April and your new best friend, Rose, has become an unlikely friend of mine. I am not sure why, but she seems to like me. Four months have passed since you cut me down to size when she runs into me in the dining hall. She blurts out an invite to coffee, then blushes like her mouth made the decision independently of her brain. I like that she isn't afraid of you enough to write me off.

Over spicy chais, she invites me to a ritual burning of ex-related items she and her friends are throwing at the Divinity School later that evening. I'm scared it'll be a trap. I'm scared you'll be there. I gently decline, but I love that she is the kind of person who would organize such an event. We grow close, drink pink lemonade on the floor of her massive basement single, listen to Phoebe Bridgers on vinyl, avoid talking about you.

Until one night, when we've just gotten back to mine after a night of party hopping, she swallows hard and she says she has something to tell me.

I think the way she treated you was really shitty. And she knows I feel that way. There's just a lot you don't know.

I learn *he*—the new boy—was with you long before I was. I learn that after my breathless confession, your friends, including Rose, told you not to do it. You said you wouldn't. You said you'd let me down easy. You said you wanted to preserve our friendship.

Three days later, you told me you were mine.

Rose confronted you. She asked why you'd do this when you already had him, when you knew you wanted him, when you knew you'd never let him go.

I don't know, you said to her. *I just woke up one morning and thought, dating Mia would be fun. So I decided to try it out for a little while.*

*

It is late January. As I stand in line at the dining hall, I feel you looking at me. Your eyes are angry. I wish you would approach me. Say anything. When I come out of the kitchen with my pizza, you are gone. I wish I could feel relief, but I am itching for a confrontation. I just know better than to initiate.

Monique told me they saw you with him the other night, at a jazz concert. I am not surprised. You do not know how to be alone. You are looking for someone to love everywhere, all the time, but you cannot handle reciprocity.

You do not know how to be happy. You destroy beautiful things because you don't think you deserve them. You pursue joy knowing it will never stop running away. It is the thrill of the chase that excites you.

You do not care about the people you hurt. You live solely for your own pleasure. I wish I could say I think that is an empty way to live, but I know it isn't. It is a selfish way to live, but I know you don't care, because it makes you feel whole.

How long will that last?

I check my phone. Monique and Priya have set our group chat aflame with jokes about the subaltern's speaking patterns. I smile. You have not earned the right to be angry with me.

*

Sometimes I wonder how this will change me. Will it make me more careful if I shield my heart and try to avoid being hurt again? Will it make me more reckless if I throw myself at others hoping to taste you on their lips? The body cannot sustain this hunger. I think of your saliva, of wiping it off my mouth like chalk from a blackboard after you pulled your lips away. Messy. Sweet. Erased. The body cannot sustain this hunger.

*

I now go days without seeing you, which is good. But occasionally I catch a glimpse of your hair from across the lobby of the Spanish department. It doesn't floor me like it once did, the stringy dull brown cropped short at your chin when we met, now hanging just past your shoulders, tucked beneath that black beret you think makes you look cultured.

When we met, my hair reached halfway down my back. Silky, shiny, black. I could do so much with it. Braids, messy buns, ponytails and pigtails, space buns, braided buns. The possibilities were paralyzing, so I cut them all away.

We are inverses now. I think maybe we always were.

*

For the record, Priya is a better kisser than you.

*

There is only one thing you ever apologize for.

Long after the end of everything, long after all the big revelations and bigger breakdowns, long after the Tweets and the blocks and the complete and utter loss of dignity, when the sun is furious and Connecticut is a sauna, I meet you for iced chais. I want us to thaw for Rose, and maybe I'm a masochist. I must be. Because you open your mouth, and you say *I'm sorry*, and just as I feel like maybe we could make it somewhere, maybe even hug, you slip the knife between my ribs: *for not realizing how invested you were.*

If it makes you feel better, you finish me off with, *I also thought my first kiss meant a lot to the other person when it didn't.*

Condensation pools between our cups. I think this is a surprising amount of effort to go to just to destroy me again. It's easy to tell when someone is afraid of themselves. I smile, and I tell you it doesn't make me feel better at all.

*

It is mid-December. I push open the door to my room and set the disc drive down on my desk. I lent it to you just days before, so you could listen to the CD I burned for you. Twenty songs. I should've known you'd run. I never learn. I feel strangely empty, strangely nothing.

Your words, only twenty minutes old, reverberate inside my skull.

You know when you really really really want something to work, but you just don't feel anything?

My knees give out.

Oh, I think, as I sink to the floor. *So this is what it is.*

I am a storyteller. I thought you knew this about me. I thought you would understand why I write what I write, why I post what I post. And yet you text me, angry. You don't want me to be telling this story. But I am a storyteller. I tell stories. And this one is mine to tell.

*

I am standing in the backyard of a run-down white house holding a red cup that used to be filled with white wine, because I am a cliché. It is the second week of my first semester of college and I don't know a single person here. Everything is muted by smoke from the fire pit and the art students' cigarettes. But the feelings I am feeling are vivid, technicolor bright. The air crackles with potential. Or maybe I am drunk.

The girl I met outside on the front porch while waiting to be let in has left me, undoubtedly bored by the painful small talk. I tilt back my head, swallow the last drops of sour liquid left in the cup.

Hey. I turn, and porch girl is back. *I brought a friend.*

You look at me, smile, extend a pale hand.

Hi, you say. *I'm—*

RAIN

I'm a little in love with everyone who looks a little like you. I wrote this in my notebook when I saw a girl on the train who I kept sneaking glances at because I swore it was you. She was so confused. I think she wanted to say something to me but neither of us were prepared for that kind of breach. Thank god. I wonder how long it'll be until I can see someone with bangs and freckles and dimples and not feel unsteady, the way a train bathroom feels while you're splashing water on your face.

I read poetry now. A lot of it. I read it so I'll know how to write about you, but also so I'll know how to write about all the girls that come after you. There's already been one. I loved her, too. Maybe more. I'm not sure yet. I do know I knew her better. But she was scared for so long. She was scared, and you made me a coward. Or maybe it's not fair to deflect the blame. Maybe I just used up all my bravery on you.

I went out drinking three days after I ruined things with the girl that came after you. When I woke up in the morning, my body was a desert. I called my sister three times but she never answered. My name is just hers with the middle removed. When I am close to the edge of something strong, I call her because I want to hear from a stranger. I was a desert and I wanted my sister because I thought she had all the answers. She was always the real artist.

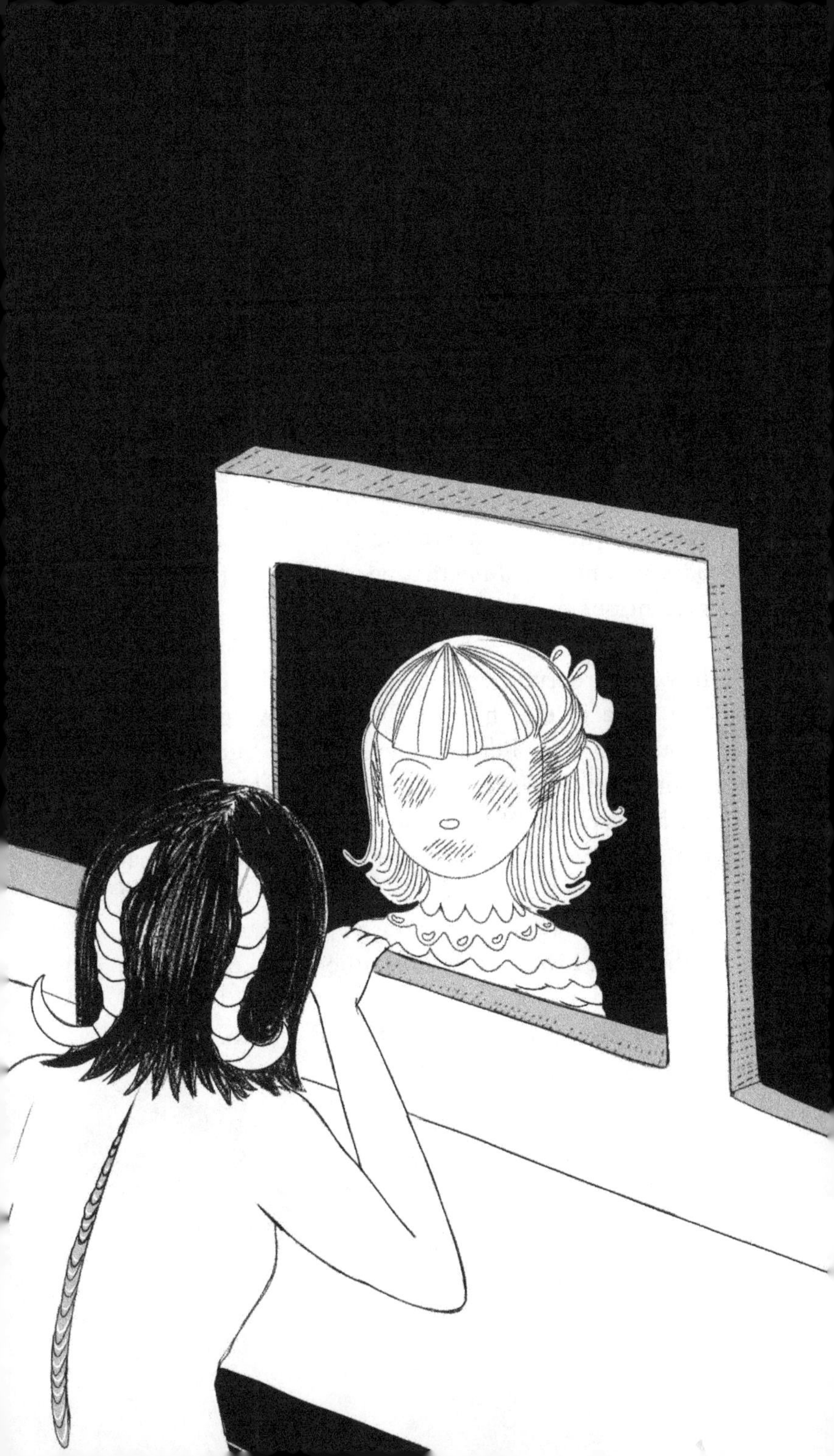

I am just her with the middle removed. I don't know why I thought she could tell me why I couldn't remember the night before. I expect too much of her. I think she hates me, a little.

There's an old note in my phone where I compare you to *train stations at night / the yellow sulfur lighting / swallowed at the edge by the midnight dark* and another where I compare you to *a soft dream*, and I dare anyone to tell me that poetry isn't all just weird pretentious bullshit.

It was February when I walked into a church for the first time in eleven years. It was snowing but not enough to stick. I don't believe in God, but I believe in my grandparents, and I don't think they can hear me if I'm not in church. They're temperamental like that. I spent the weekend drinking with the girl that came after you, because we were both still scared of each other. I told them about you, and her, and my father, and I think they understood. I asked them to try to make things warm for me. When I stepped outside again, the snow had turned to rain.

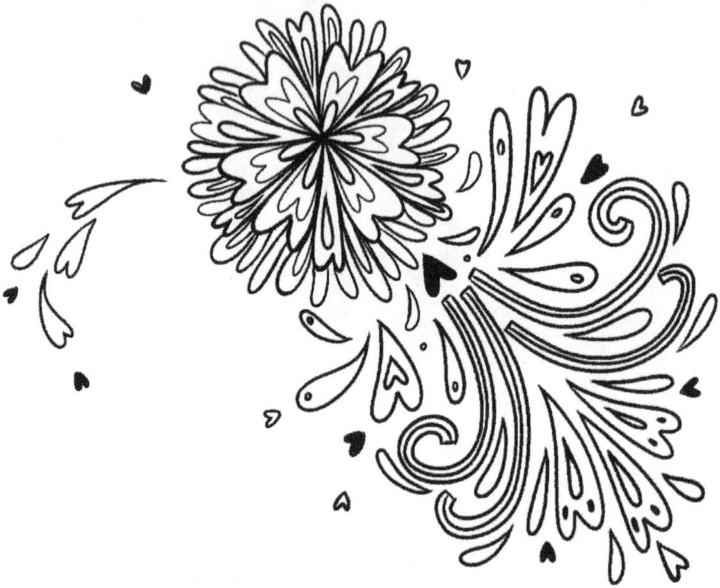

I WANT TO BE ON THE GOLDEN STATE WARRIORS DANCE TEAM

even though a girl I knew in college once said I move like my body and mind have two different ideas about where I should be going because I want to roll my chest for an audience and smash the soles of my sneakers into the ground in sync with twenty-two sister shoes and I want to be essential and if I were hundreds of miles away at last belonging to the city where I was born I'd wrap my sequins around my lovers in the indigo hours and stroll into dives in the castro postgame sweaty and shining and I'd point to the tv behind the bar and tell them *didyouknowIamhereforyourentertainment* and you would only ever know me onscreen a dancing dyke in blue and gold instead of breathing all my hope into you and what I never told you is that kissing you feels like watching Andre Iguodala make both of his free throws (AN ACT OF GOD) and loving you feels like Klay Thompson trying to finish game six of the 2019 nba finals with a torn acl: this is what I was born to do even though it hurts.

MELATONIN DREAMS

i.

The house is in New Haven, I think. I can tell by the wide and quiet streets, the elm trees in full green. This is the first sign of unreality— in the waking world you have never been anywhere I am. It's funny, though, that it's the same building every time. I wonder from which subliminal corner of my mind it came, because it's definitely not somewhere I've been before. There's a yellow porch swing. There's only one floor. The house moves from city to city depending on the night (New York Baltimore McAllen Philadelphia Iowa City Boston when will it stop when will it fucking stop). But for a millisecond, when I stand on the sidewalk in the dregs of sun (the sky is always lavender when I go looking for you) and look up the gently sloping hill at the front door, the way the light cracks open and spills gold over the roof is so gently and unquestionably New Haven. I must have passed this house on one of my many aimless walks through East Rock that I'd take as an alternative to my dorm room's fifth floor windows (the easy way out) and just not noticed it then. It's brown and dark green, earthy and long like a sideways shotgun and I'm ready for you to blow my head off again.

ii.

Your room is messy tonight. Wood-paneled this time. Yellow lampglow, we're gay, it could never be the overhead. Plush black rug, bare walls, dirty clothing everywhere. It doesn't feel like you, but it's where you are. I slide under grey sheets to lay beside you. You're fully clothed. Suddenly, I am not. Tears run down your cheeks. You tell me about something awful that has happened to you, someone you've lost. I won't be more specific— even when you're a figment I still can't bear to wring you out entirely. I know it doesn't seem that way. I know what you think of me. All I can say is you're the only person I loved enough to still preserve a modicum of their privacy. I am still trying to protect you from the rage of everyone who wants me to be happy. I hold your jaw like glass. I kiss salt. Your teeth graze my neck. Bruise. I missed your calluses, your smoke, your silver chain. I wonder if you let her see this side of you. I wonder if placing yourself in my arms is your way of admitting you were wrong. Your fingers curve into me, scoop out my desire like pomegranate seeds. You keep your boxers on.

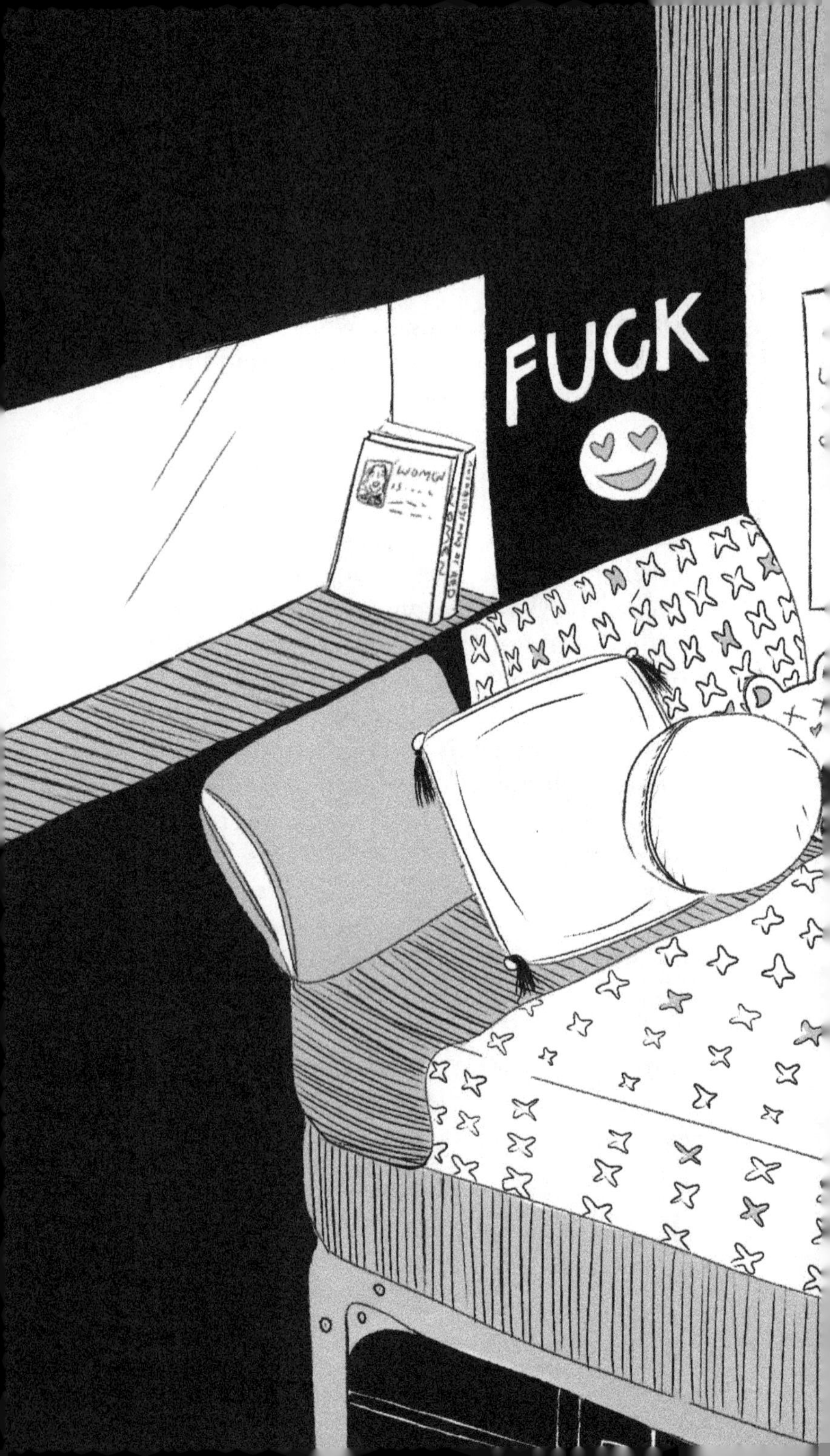
FUCK

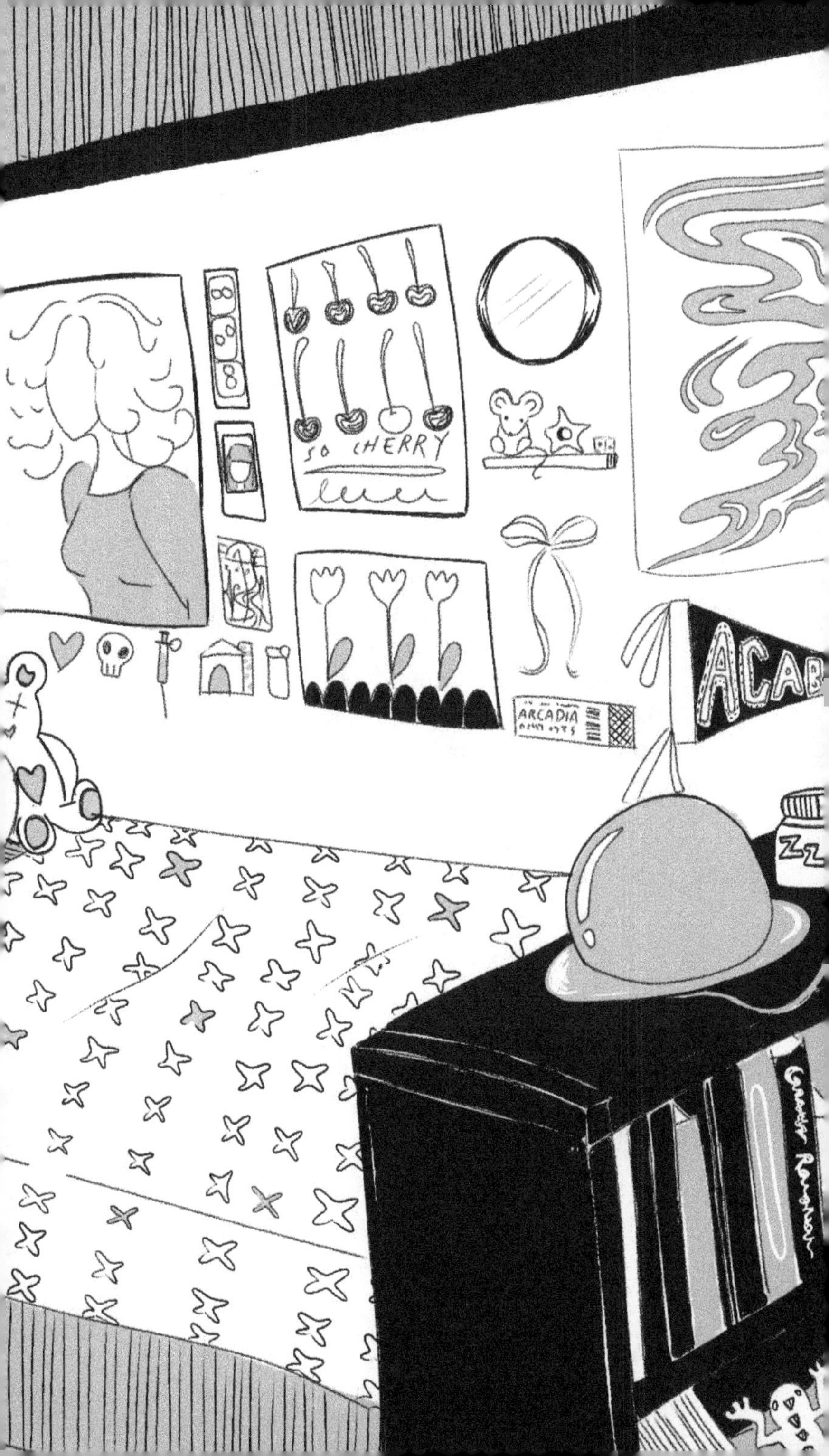
SO CHERRY
ARCADIA

iii.

In this house, you have your own bathroom. I pee with the door open so I can still see you. I know if my line of sight is interrupted I'll jump somewhere else instantly and I'm not ready to lose you yet. (Will I ever be?) It's been a long time since my brain has let me come back here. I stopped taking these for a reason. But I was tired. I'm always so fucking tired. I figured a minor devastation would be worth the extra sleep. I'm still peeing and listening to you recite a Hanif Abdurraqib quote you read about grief that reminds you of *that intense period of our lives* and I know I was wrong. This devastation won't be minor, and it won't ever be worth it. I know where we are but this is not the kind of lucid where I can save myself. It's hell to be trapped behind my own eyes, letting you happen to me when I'm supposed to have control here— all of this is me, isn't it? I should be able to stop it. Instead I hover, agonized. I can't stop the black, I can't make you real, I can't make you stay. As I stumble back to your bed, I feel the edges melting. Your voice reaches for me but it's static. I know I'm running out of time. When my eyes open I won't be able to remember the sound of your voice and I will shatter. I try to call for you, I try to hang on tight, I want to smash my fists against your bedroom door and beg *not again not again not again not again* but I wake anyway. Your name and salt—mine this time—stinging the cracks in my lips.

ANYWHERE WITH YOU COULD BE NEW YORK

When I close my eyes I am in your bed again. I am lying on those wrinkled grey sheets and you are making me feel. I think maybe you like me, a little. You should know I remember things. The feather-lightness with which you touched my arm, after, leaning back on the mattress in your Twin Peaks shirt. Your pulse, pounding against my hand through your skin. You held me there like I kept your heart beating. Do you understand what I kept leaving behind for you and your little life in the most racist city in America? Per Google, so if you have a problem you can take it up with them. But somehow I still fell in love with the edges you smoothed down, the used bookstores where we were so irresponsible, the liquor store where you bought that $12 bottle of Cabernet Sauvignon with the atom on the label I have been searching for ever since, the winding residential streets all blue in the twilight where you got us lost on purpose. I string your promises across the weeks before I see you again and I hang tight. I think today could be the day I take you to the best Vietnamese restaurant in the state, or the butterfly conservatory in the Natural History Museum, or the bookstores I have been keeping in a running list on my phone. Before I know it, I am running back to you again. I moved to the city that never sleeps to become my own giant and what am I doing? I am kissing you hundreds of miles away as you cry over your cowardice in the bright winter morning. I am telling you it's okay to flay me. I am walking you out of my life and the sun is warm on my back and I am telling you if you change your mind, if you move to New York like you said you were planning, the door will always be open and I know I am the problem. How will you learn? If you don't choose me, you should lose me. But if you could make Davis Square glitter like the West Village I can only imagine how you would transform the end of the line. I am not in the business of ultimatums and I have never made demands of you but now I am asking: What about me? What about *me?*

LONGING DISTANCE

Since August 2019, I have been falling exclusively and regularly for women who live in cities that aren't mine. Under skies of different blues, powder, navy, midnight, I stand in Connecticut ready to be changed. I stand waiting, watching for the $28 sanctuary others call the BoltBus. I am on the edge and I am breaking my life to get to you because that is what I do for what I love. I am held in the claustrophobic womb of peeling leather seats for two and a half hours at a time and I curl into myself and I touch the feral creature of my heart and ask *is there anything left to give* and it howls *yes yes yes forever.*

But you already know this story well. I'm sure you're still there, now, expecting, because these are the roles we play. It's easy to be you, one hundred forty-three-point-three miles away. It's easy to be the one waiting, the one from whom nothing is expected other than existence when the bus pulls into the station.

I become an expert at traveling light. I stretch one lipstick across several outfits. I only bring one book. When I settle my head against the greasy bus window, I let my home fall away, feeling nothing at all. I have learned that I am very good at leaving my life and very bad at returning to it. I wonder if that says something about how I was living before you. In the hours and days after a visit, everything that used to be life-endingly important feels so shimmeringly false. I vibrate through my tissue-paper life, restless with the knowledge that if I really wanted, at any moment I could be gone. At any moment, I could walk out of class, take the blue line to the station, and hold you in my eyes before dinner. I rip out my roots from New Haven and begin to plant them in you, even though you never said I could, even though I didn't ask. The walls of my once-beloved dorm room are suffocating. I pace up and down the streets of this barely-city wishing for your skyscrapers to make me feel small again.

We can never truly belong to two places. They say when I run to you I am giving up too easily, but the truth is that I tried. I tried so hard for so long, but this place sees all of me, all the time, and it is unforgiving. It's cruel with my dreams, tears them limb from limb as I watch, powerless. The breaking is so frequent I no longer have time to rebuild before it happens again. Maybe it's true, maybe I'm running, but I'm not giving up. I'm trying to survive.

But you have hurt me, too. With you, the pain is always worse because I take the bus to leave this all behind but here it is again, following me one hundred forty-three-point-three miles away and pressing its sharp blade against my neck until I admit that no matter where I go, I can't escape something that lives inside me. I am my own hurt, I must be, because how can so many places be wrong at once? So here I am again, curled catatonic around my laptop, empty wine bottles standing at attention on the floor by my bed frame, failing to numb that pure bright pain. So here I am and I lean in. I tell myself that unlike in New Haven, with you, everything fades. The hurt does not compound itself; I don't have to live inside it. The hurt has no agenda, no intention but to clear eventually. So until then, I breathe in, I breathe out, and it fades, and I'm back on the bus, and the people who say they love me ask in horror, *Why do you keep doing this to yourself?*

I don't quite know what they mean. Are they asking about the constant torture that comes with the pursuit of a long-distance relationship? The chasing of someone too far away to love me back the way I want? Or is it the simple action of the investment itself, the wasted weekends, the missed parties and study groups and time with friends? Regardless, I'm shocked they even ask, because everyone knows I am too much. Everyone knows I love loud and deep and it scares people away. It destroys everything before I get a chance to feel it.

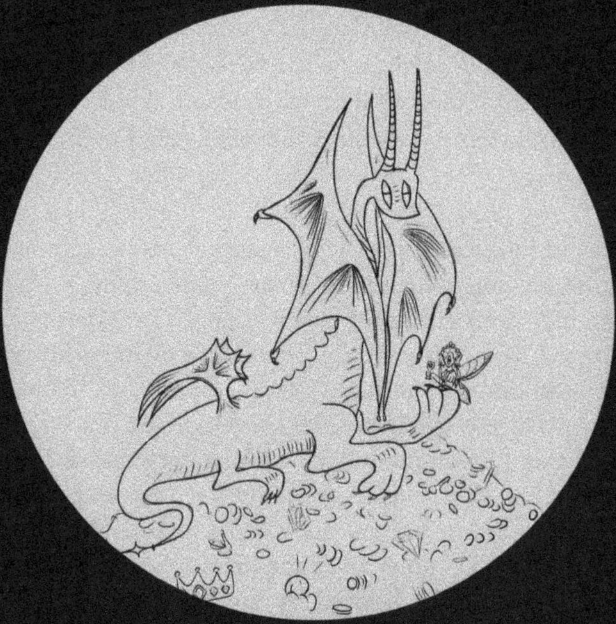

The distance protects us from my disgusting, destructive excess. This way, I don't have to try to turn it off, hating myself when I inevitably fail. This way, I can give of myself in small doses. This way, you only get what you can handle. I might not get to have the slow, sure domesticity that I've always craved, the kind that can only grow from proximity and time, but I still get to have you.

It's pointless, and that's what makes it perfect. It's one hundred forty-three-point-three impossibilities that can hide every half-truth you whisper to me. That I am wanted. That you are ready. That there's no one who can stand in our way. You aren't here with me, but the way you make me feel is pushing itself up and out of my throat and blooming into something everyone in New Haven can look at and say *she's in love*. You aren't here with me, and so I can create you for myself. The you I imagine would hold my hand in public. The you I imagine would be beloved by my friends. The you I imagine would watch *Frances Ha* in my twin XL with me and walk me to class even when yours isn't on the way and bring me oat chais and kiss my forehead when I get the way I do at this time of year, when I'm behind on work and I can't wake up early and my brain is whispering all those mean and untrue things, and remind me that I am doing just fine. The you I imagine does not exist, but what I have made becomes real to me, and that you is perfect. You want to do these things, you do. The only thing stopping you is one bus ride.

For the real you, this separation is an uncrossable divide. There's nothing for it, so I say *I understand* even though I've crossed it for you time and time again. Nothing can hold me back from the giving, the thinning, the eviscerating. The emptying of myself, the turning over of all I am to you. Somehow I could never think of it as sacrifice, even as I tenderly set a part of myself beside you each time before I leave, a part I will try but never be able to regrow. I still think it's what I ought to do. I have to know I tried. I have to know there is nothing more I could have given you, nothing that could have made you less afraid.

You have a life here, my friend begs me over the phone. It's the last time and I don't know it's the last time. I'm walking to the train to the bus that will take me back to her and I don't want to hear this because *here* means New Haven and *here* means *without you* and we've reached the point where I no longer know what such a thing would mean for me. *You have friends. You have a whole publication. And every time you go there, you're putting your entire life on hold. You can't do this anymore.*

I stop in the sun. I let myself feel warm. The air comes whirling off the Charles River, thick and bright. I breathe in, and I breathe out, and I am back in Connecticut, and I am miles away from home, and I can feel you everywhere.

CRAVE *After Paramore*

Just for a second it all felt simple, I'm already missing it
So I crave, crave to do it again, all again.
  —Paramore, "Crave"

Crave:

To see things through to the end. To muzzle my optimism. To focus on my breath. To take care of myself—to drink more water, to take a multivitamin once in a while. To keep the wave of panic from crashing every time I open a Google Doc. To own my words rather than fear them. To need less from you. To fix my bottom teeth. To read a 600-page hard fantasy novel. To watch the bleak-branched trees of two, three, four wintergrey states speed past the window of a northbound train. To stop cracking in half when I remember how you said, *Imagine emotions as a huge wave that's headed to shore—I'm riding it, but you're drowning.*

To ride the red line across the Charles River under powder blue October skies. To give you what you want. To fetishize uncertainty; to thrive in the grey areas. To buy your roommate another six pack of Lagunitas as an apology for all the four AM laughter. To stop rereading your text about missing the four AM laughter. To cry in every Cambridge square one last time—Davis, Central, Inman, Harvard—and *know* it's the last time. To take you at face value. To claim your throat with purple promises. To stop missing you when you're right here.

To read your mind. To know the rules. To know when they were about to change on me. To be so infallible as to be blameless. To never give you a reason.

To reread Chloé Caldwell on the E train when my legs itch to be led astray—*The long version is: that's what my entire twenties felt like; Wanting. Yearning. Craving. Constant craving.*

To make you into a villain. To make it easier on myself. To keep pretending I don't understand. To be crueler in Washington Square Park. To take off my sunglasses in Washington Square Park. To force you to confront my pain, to take a little responsibility. To explain that I can't recategorize you in my heart just because you want to break your woman and have her too, and that this doesn't make me callous, and that this doesn't make you irredeemable. To make peace with deflation. To let things die. To leave well enough alone. To tell myself it's possible you could miss me, too.

To keep the promise I made to myself to never write about you, because you deserve better. To admit I only made this promise because once in bed you admitted you hoped you'd *earn an essay* and I wanted to deny you *something*. To admit part of why I write is to punish. To kill this childish revenge fantasy. To find a middle ground.

To take the advice a professor gave me five years ago, when I begged her to help me stop writing about my first love: *Imagine her as a ghost hovering at the edges of your work. Acknowledge her, thank her, and let her haunt every page.*

To have met you after your outline crystallized. To be patient; to save you for later. To give us a fightless chance.

To grab your head between my hands and make you face your stagnation. To take my own advice. To stop wanting to be the reason you set yourself free. To tell you that actually, maybe *you* need a new therapist.

To sip bourbon gingers at KGB without looking over shoulders for a false memory. To beat my record for how fast I can make you come (three minutes—not bad). To rip the pen from your hand as you wrote us on the wall. To listen to Maggie Rogers and scream when she screams *all I ever wanted is to make something FUCKING LAST*. To lay in McCarren Park on the first warm day of the year silently smoking in the sun with Morgan; to feel for the first time like I'm ready to stop running from New York. To stop offering my neck to the blade. To accept you were right about my chest feeling lighter without you. To hold back the tears because you could've been wrong, if you wanted to be. To kiss you shrouded in steel. To take you like we're teenagers in the backseat of my Subaru. To lay out on the frozen bank of the Hudson the day after Christmas, my face and coat wide open to the anemic sun while you take me apart with shivering hands, the only sounds the soft crackle and slush of ice sheets scraping across each other, the caws of migratory birds overhead, your breath. *To do it again, all again.*

THE WOMAN WHO KNOWS

In the dream, you let me down just like all the years before. I know you like I know the insides of my eyelids. Still, I'm ready for you to surprise me. Just in case. In the dream it's someone's friend's birthday. Someone with a job title so vaguely official it sounds fictional and a fluorescent apartment with a massive astroturf balcony suspended in the Midtown glitter-bomb. I should be feigning festivity and wine literacy from the comfort of the white suede couch. Instead I'm immobilized outdoors, waiting for a text from you that'll never come. I lean my hips against the railing as rain slices through me. Over the edge, an infinite obsidian plummet. I tilt my head back, dip my hair into the storm. In the dream you promised you'd *make time* before you left the city. (I know it's a dream because it's my city, not yours.) But I cried the night before, knees straddling your lap, hips bucking around your indifferent fingers. I tilted my head back. Forced my tears to slide sideways off my cheeks and into my ears. All sounds muted and I pretended we were underwater. I wanted you there in the silence with me. I wanted one moment where our Venn diagrams of truth became a circle. But more than that I wanted—still want—to see you happy, and they say death by drowning is euphoric right before the black. I always know it's coming. I always know before you do.

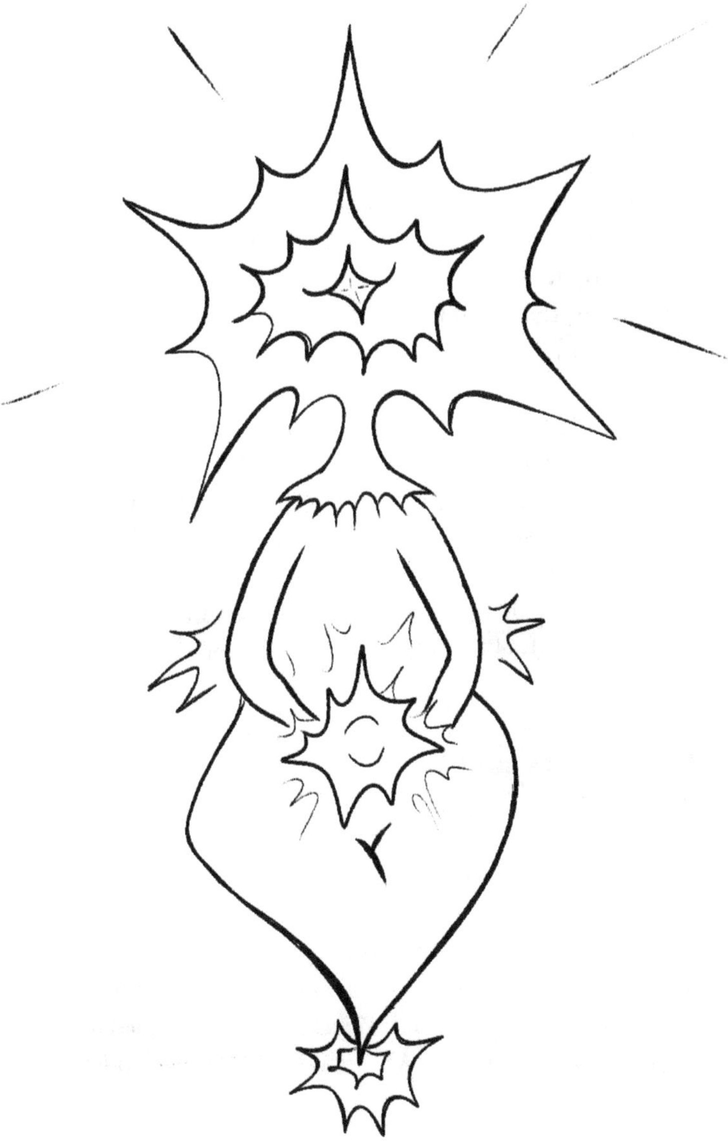

VENICE

The pocket of your hoodie is still full of sand from our nighttime trip to the beach. No – you said it's my hoodie now. I certainly earned it. The hoodie is massive, fleece-lined, grey. It's not a piece of clothing I have to worry about. I wear it to clean my apartment or cook something that might splatter. We all need something we aren't afraid to ruin.

The hoodie has traveled three months and 3000 miles and yet, tiny translucent grains still stick to my phone's black rubber case when I pull it out to check the time, to look for your name in a text I now know isn't coming, to read my lock screen like a prayer. It's been the same for five years. A pale hand pointing forward into a blooming, black-and-white field. Nine words overlaid:

Start over
You can if you want
No biggie

It's been three months and 3000 miles since we ignored all our little incompatibilities to clamber up the dunes at the edge of the continent. You offered your hand like a gentleman to pull me up each time my boots sank into the damp. We laid on our backs and watched the airplanes take off from LAX. Hoods up. Hands hidden.

Acutely aware of every single inch between us. So many, but still not enough to break the charge. I pointed to the blinking red lights in the sky and asked where you thought they were going. I hoped you'd say somewhere far away like Prague or Thailand. *I don't know. San Francisco, maybe.* You wouldn't play along, even then, when it no longer mattered. We used to unfurl when we were together. The hurt and distance have made us strangers. Silence. Sand. The ocean was black and still. I couldn't stop looking at the stars. You couldn't stop looking at me.

Earlier, in the passenger seat of your Subaru:

Will you take me to the beach?

Of course I'll take you to the beach.

The only promise you've ever kept.

We drove to your house first. You said it would be cold by the water. I chose the Costa Azul Surf Shop hoodie because it was bigger and I wanted to feel held. Even straight from your closet it didn't smell like you. I snooped through your bookshelves. You insisted it meant something that we were both reading *Eileen* at the same time. I wanted to beg you to stop making meaning when you'd already euthanized the idea of us. I didn't understand why you wouldn't let me go. I realize now that you didn't either.

I thought it was sweet that you were so nervous it took you three tries to pull into your driveway. Somehow, I still didn't think you'd ever want to kiss me again after what I said to you. So when I got into your car, my lips were red. On the beach, suddenly, they weren't. Now yours were, lips and chin and the corners of your mouth smudged with an accidental brand of sorts. I decided to claim you just this once, even if you'd never claim me.

You slipped your hands beneath my jacket. You were always searching for my warmth. I was your vacation. You were my meteor. You were always siphoning me into you and I just stood there and let you do it. You know how I am. Desperate for a concrete ending to our narrative arc. A tidy end to a fucked-up waste. Just so tired of blowing everything to pieces. This was a rare chance to put it back together one more time before I let it go. Leave on a high note. The air cleared. Our shit addressed. I'm glad you could meet me here. I hoped you would. I've decided not to miss you after this. You are going to set me free.

When you kissed me the ocean swelled and crashed behind us. I thought, just for a frame, about taking your hand and walking, then running, then diving. I thought about how cold it would be, how dark.

Would you finally see me if I were floating in the black, flickering out in front of you?

UNIDENTIFIED AERIAL PHENOMENON OVER MANHATTAN AVENUE

I walked down the street where you used to live tonight. I haven't done that since you left. The scaffolding still coats the building next door in forest green and shadow. I stood outside the door where you had greeted me just three times and smoked a quarter of a j. Three times was enough to form an emotional attachment to scaffolding – like most lesbians our intimacy grew exponentially. Nobody came in or out of the building. I wasn't there long, maybe eight minutes, *though* (as you once said) *it always feels much longer* whenever it comes to you. I looked up to see a trio of girls walking in my direction, braced against the wind and dressed to go OUT, and I blew a stream of smoke into the wind. I was wearing lipstick – I know you're probably wondering. I went around the corner and down the block to the sidewalk in front of the bodega where, less than twelve hours before your flight away from me forever, I twisted both ankles simultaneously. I was wearing my three-inch platform wedges that always endanger my life but I always risk it because of how good they make my legs look. I almost ate it, but you caught me. You grabbed my arms as my legs buckled and I swore loudly in front of a three year old child on a scooter and his father. *I'm sorry*, I gasped, cheeks burning,

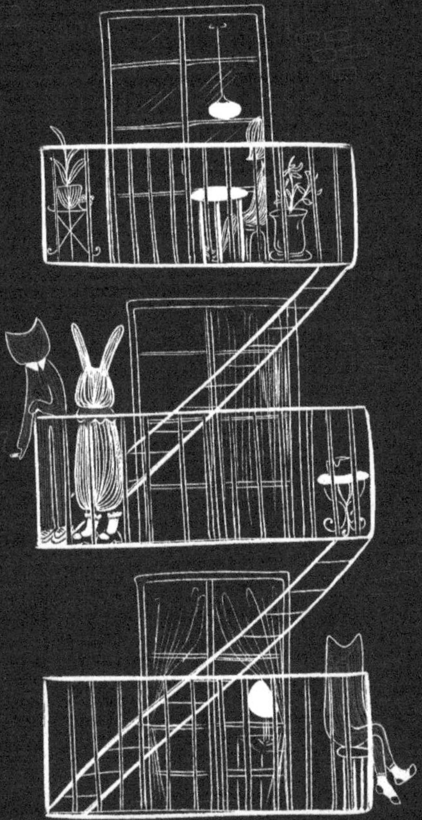

but the father shrugged. *It's New York! Very graceful, by the way.* Only now did I register your arms around my waist and the fact that it was broad daylight but you were holding me in public and you were smiling. You had this sense of my body as an object in space that I don't even have about myself, and I *live* here. You could anticipate my trajectories, always grab my hands wrists waist long before I hit the ground. In bed this manifested as something incredibly erotic, your unique ability to get *me* of all people to *slow down*, let the tension rise like magma in the pit of my stomach until I would do anything for your hands. My ankles were recovered but my legs were still jelly because that was what your desire did to me, and I wasn't expecting that. Tonight, though, your door won't swing open. You won't be standing there in a ribbed tank and boy shorts with that stupid vape in your hand and that gorgeous smile on your face to welcome me in. That smile could outshine the lights on the Kosciuszko Bridge. That smile splashes an aurora across the sky. For ten more minutes on the roof with you the night we saw the pulsing, shifting glow shining through the clouds above Greenpoint and it became our psychological burden to bear *together*, the night I turned and looked into your eyes and finally understood the thread that bound us – you and I just *want to believe*, for five more minutes, one, I'd give it all.

LETTER TO AN OLD ARCHITECT

You think you're a good person because you won't punch me in the stomach.
—boygenius

Black windows and snow, so much snow, whipping past me in the dark on the train home from D.C. You are at the other end of the Northeast Regional, out for a run even in the ice. I sit there biting my lip in the Quiet Car, imagining that through my headphones you're telling me everything you want to do to me. Eyes closed, I can see the snow stuck in your curls, the red January glow of your skin. Over text you say you're *invigorated*. You say we should try it together, running in the wind and sting. I respond *Absolutely not*. I know my limits. This is the last time I will recognize them with you.

*

When I meet you I'm 22, living with my mother and working three jobs, one full-time in corporate that wants me dead. I just started writing a novel that has yet to find its legs. I do not know myself and still think I can find her in other women. Women like you. You're 25, living in a different city, in graduate school for architecture (though what you'd really like to do is build large-scale abstract sculptures). I am enchanted by your smile, your gentle masculinity, our easy chemistry. After our second date, I convince you to call me on the phone. You resist, you say you hate phone calls, but it becomes our best form of communication. We talk for hours. You want to know everything about my bleak romantic past and make it no secret that you want to join the roster of heartbreak. You want me to write about you, which is refreshing to hear. (That's how I know you'll be okay with this, even when it gets ugly.) I am someone who stumbles and falls on my face in love. I'm arrogant enough to assume I've split enough lips by now to know how to avoid the sidewalk cracks, the tree roots. I can make it work. I can do better this time. You just have to want it, too.

I shouldn't have had to beg. You were lucky I was ever yours at all.

*

I wake up on the first day of the new year to you in my bed. I have known you for a little over a month. You wait till after I make you come again in the bright morning to ask what I want from this. I deflect, ask you back. You won't let it go. You push and prod and invoke your therapist (who, you said, told you that it's okay for emotional investment to be imbalanced in a relationship as long as both parties are kind about it) until you finally get me to admit *I want to be with you, in a real way.*

You sigh. *That's sweet.*

I should have ended it then.

You tell me you can't be in a relationship with me. You tried long distance before, it didn't go well, you aren't ready to try again. But you really like me. You'll come back to New York, and I already have tickets to see you in two weeks, and I can come visit whenever. *Maybe we can... just see each other when we're in each other's cities,* you say. *I just can't do long distance, you know?*

Okay, I say, still wrapped in your arms. Your grip feels suffocating now instead of safe. *Sure.*

Do you still want to come visit?

I wish I could want anything else.

*

You text me, *one of the first things I told my therapist about you was that I felt like you just really Saw me immediately and we just like... saw each other.*

I love our hours-long phone calls about niche internet drama and video games and general lesbian acceleration. I love your sweetness, when you want to be sweet. I love reading your books at the table in your huge sunny kitchen while you cook for me: shakshuka, Japanese curry, white bean pasta with arrabiata sauce. I love laying on your couch with my head in your lap, slightly stoned in the midmorning light, while you play video games and explain the rules to me. I love standing next to you at your roommate's show and making eye contact and I love that you know, without me needing to speak, that as soon as his set ends we won't stay for the next two bands, we'll sprint back to your apartment in the cold so you can fuck me as loud as we want before he comes home.

Sometimes during sex, you confess once, *my brain just goes: TELL THEM YOU LOVE THEM.*

You never do. You say plenty else. You beg me *please* you call me *baby* you whine my name, stuttering in ecstasy. No one ever has before.

One afternoon, you text that you might not be able to make our scheduled call later because you aren't feeling well. I am disappointed but I understand. I know your life is more demanding. You act like our age and life gap is insurmountable, or at least enough for you to hold your adulthood over me. Sometimes you're right. I tell myself to remember you've been through a specific kind of hell I never have and never will. I understand that I'll never understand. I refuse to make that mistake again. So I reply that it's okay, no pressure if not, I just want you to feel better.

With that, you switch, for the first of many times.

Do you even want to? You don't seem very interested.

Your anger surprises me. I try to backtrack. Of course I want to talk to you, I was trying not to pressure you, I have been taking SSRIs for over a year and I know how the brain can drag someone under, how just a phone call can feel like an anvil on the chest. You double down. My "nonchalance" makes you "feel bad." If you want space, you "will communicate that" – I "won't have to guess." Desperate, I type rapid apologies, six messages in a row. I'll do anything to keep you, so I become an expert at those three little words: *I'm so sorry.*

You call me. I hear your voice, thick and sad, and all I want to do is make it better, so I say them again.

That night, hours later, you text me: *it's late and I'm feeling sappy but I'm glad we got to talk earlier today :) I prob don't say it enough but I really like hearing your voice*

As my heart rate settles, I let your sweetness wipe away the anxiety. When Morgan asks how things are going, I don't tell her about the earlier texts. I'm used to losing myself in the people I fall for, but this is the furthest it has ever gone. It should terrify me, but I am in deep enough to ignore it.

By the end of everything, it'll feel like all I ever did was apologize to you. I was always doing something wrong, breaking a rule I never knew about. These days, when I think of you, the primary emotion I remember is not love – it's guilt.

*

When things are good, they're great. When they're bad, they're disastrous. You have a remarkable capacity to turn me into an enemy. The more time I spend with you, the more I find myself somehow on the other side of an argument I didn't realize we were having. You are volatile, unpredictable. You assume worst intentions, twist my jokes and compliments into insults. You are so determined to misread me and I don't know why. Pushing me off with a glare when I kiss down your neck in bed, then two breaths later: *You never initiate sex, and it makes me feel awful.* I have initiated almost every single time, from our first kiss on the bench in Tompkins Square Park to five minutes ago. *I don't understand, I'm so confused,* I must have said this a million times, *what did I do, tell me what I did so I can fix it.*

All I ever did was want you.

You didn't do anything wrong, you always say in such a dead and sullen tone, and forgive me if I don't exactly find that convincing. I wonder if you have done this to anyone else before. A sick part of me hopes it's a pattern. Otherwise, the problem is me. Just me.

*

The closer we get, the more late-night phone conversations about the nature of love, the more of your lore you reveal to me, the stronger your inclination towards punishment. You take me to a huge birthday party in your city where I know no one and immediately abandon me. It's so obvious that your roommate and all your friends make sympathetic comments to me, distancing themselves from your behavior. I end up on the back porch sharing a joint with a girl with silver glitter at the corners of her eyes who tells me she can't *believe* someone would leave a pretty girl like me all alone. Before your friends see us through the sliding glass door and practically drag you outside, I consider becoming the type of person who takes revenge. When I see your obvious indifference, the way your eyes glaze over as you take in the scene before you, I wish I'd tilted up her chin and exhaled smoke through her parted lips in time for you to see. Instead, I take your arm and let you drunkenly apologize to me in the kitchen. Nobody's perfect. How could I expect that from you? You call me *baby* over and over. You press sloppy kisses all over my face and neck until I fold. I steal a pale pink rose from the birthday girl's gift table and don't give it to you until we're in the car on the way back to your place.

For me? you gasp. *You're such a romantic.*

In the morning, when we're sober, we will fight about

how you left me. You will yell. I will cry. You will say you wanted to have morning sex and now, because of me, because I couldn't let it go, we can't.

For now, I hold your hand in the backseat and stare at you with unabashed awe. It might be twisted, but for now, I feel like the luckiest girl in the world.

At home, you put the rose in a vase with the lilies I brought you when I arrived a few days ago. By the time I leave, it will be dead.

*

You say I care too much about what things mean. Why do I need so much reassurance? Why do I need so much clarity? Why can't I just let us be what we are?

Chloé Caldwell writes, *Things lose their meaning. I am tired of things having meaning. Meaning is useless. Meaning is new-agey. Meaning means nothing.*

I love a grey area, you tell me. *Why does everything need to be defined?*

I used to be someone who squeezed significance out of every moment, every gesture, every tender word. Now I am losing faith in my ability to tell what's true. I teach myself to compartmentalize. If I decide to blanket assume your tenderness is just an act and your cruelty just the result of a brain that's been fried to hell, if I strip your actions of their meaning, I can keep myself from expecting better. I can survive a little longer.

Ari cuts off my rambling about one of our recent fights in their kitchen in D.C.: *I know you really like this person, but… she does not sound stable.*

Morgan's love and concern reaches through my phone screen all the way from New York: *You absolutely do not make anyone's life worse and i hate that she ever made you even question that about yourself!!*

Charlotte texts me from Cambridge: *I haven't had sex in three years and I STILL wouldn't choose this.*

In the past few years, my friends have stood by and let me make my mistakes, so their intense worry now rattles me. Am I becoming the kind of woman I said I'd never be?

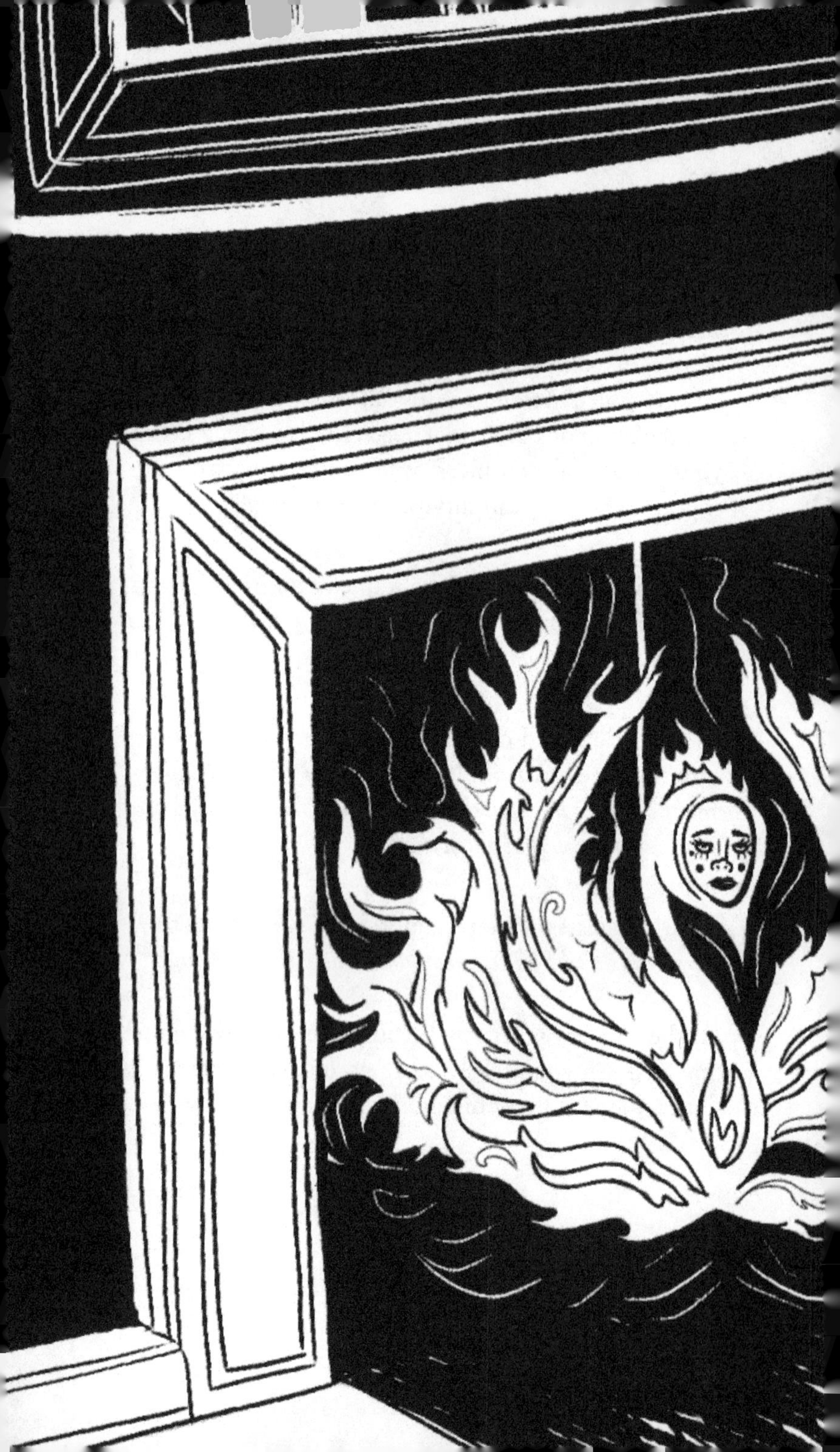

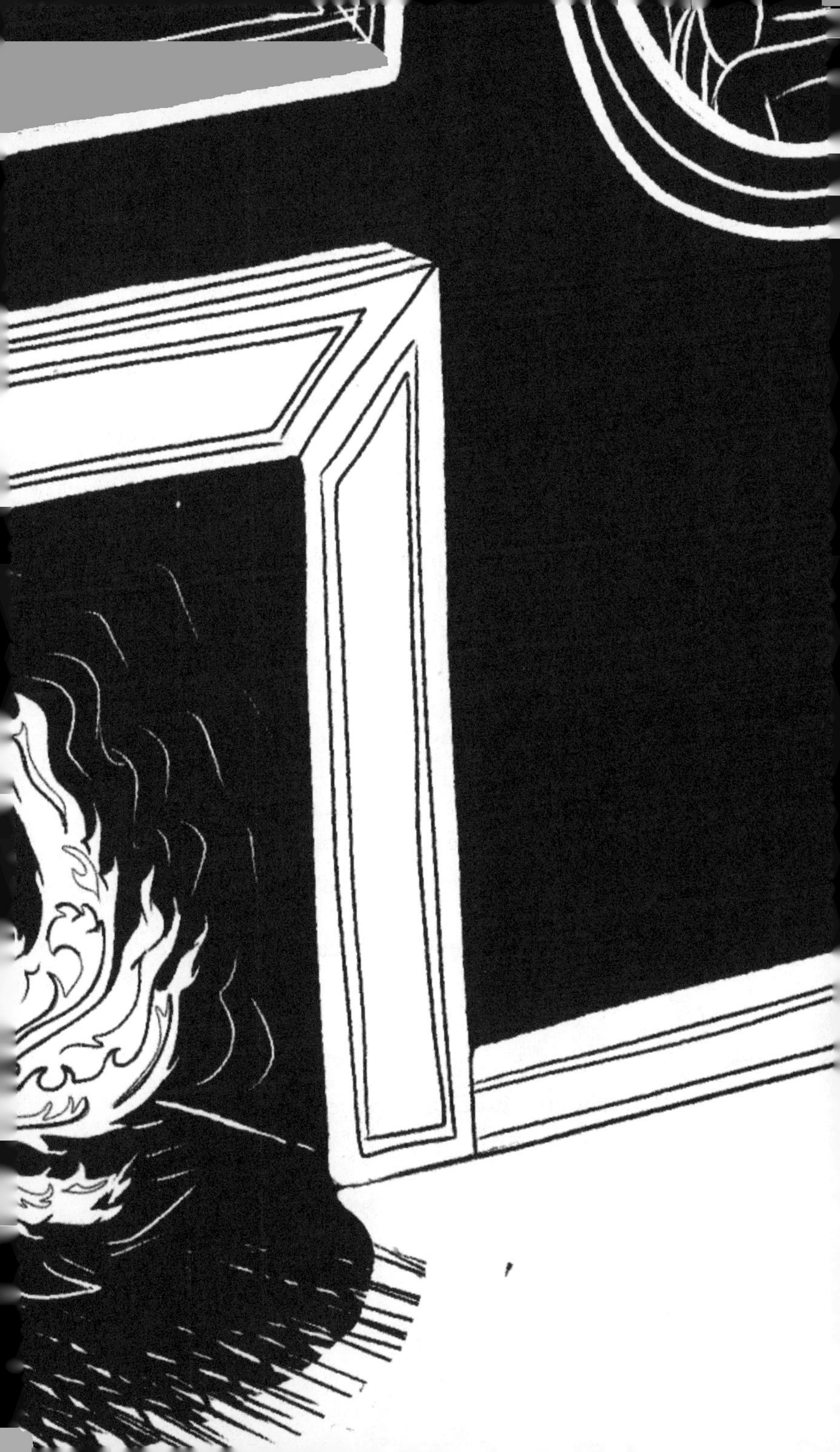

I miss your kitchen the most. The soft yellow walls, the way the air grows hazy with dust in the early morning light, coffee / wine / uncountable meals at the wooden table. Sitting on your lap wrapped in nothing but a blanket while we wait for dinner to finish cooking, kissing you as though you can satisfy my hunger.

The last time I visit (though I don't know yet it's the last time), you fall into a deep depression. I have never seen a switch so fast. My own bouts of depression are a slow slide down a steadily declined plane over a course of days, not hours. One second we're in a coffee shop near the art museum we just came from and you're plastering kisses all over my face; the next, we're in your bedroom and you're giving me the silent treatment, your face twisted in a quivering combination of anguish and annoyance. My body tenses, skin prickling with the static of a brewing confrontation. I can tell you don't want me here anymore, but you can't bring yourself to say it.

After three hours, I can't stand it. *I feel like I came to visit at a bad time. I'm sorry.*

Maybe it's too much to expect reassurance, but my heart still bruises when you sit up on your mattress and sigh. *The thing is, there's never going to be a good time.*

Oh.

You reach across me to grab your 32oz mason jar of water from your nightstand. *And with school, it's only going to get worse.*

You drink for a long time. I don't remember what I say after.

The next day, hours before I'm meant to leave, you are in a fetal position in bed facing the wall. I'm so worried about your catatonia that I postpone my trip back to New York to ensure you make it through the night. I work from your mattress beside you. You scroll through TikTok, slide your perpetually freezing hands up my shirt, try relentlessly to convince me to abandon my spreadsheets for your strap.

By the evening you've made a full recovery. You pour me red wine and cook me dinner and I kiss you up against the yellow walls of your pantry with the golden scent of frying shallots filling the air and we're back on the rollercoaster again in the part of the freefall that feels so right. We get into bed and I smell the wine on your breath as you say in the smallest, sweetest voice, *Thank you for today.*

I look into your eyes and rest a hand on your cheek. *Of course.*

When I finally get on the bus home the next morning, on Valentine's Day, I leave feeling like we're finally getting somewhere. I leave feeling like we're stronger than ever, we made it through something impossibly vulnerable and came out the other side, because this can't have meant nothing, can it?

What I don't know yet, what you'll tell me later, is that at the same moment I'm having this revelation, you're deciding it's time to burn it all.

*

Who's to say my heart didn't start breaking the moment you pulled out the chair beside me at that bookstore bar in the East Village and asked if the seat was taken? Everything comes to a head. I can see the writing on the wall but I'm pretending I can't read.

Flashes: the way your hair looks in the morning, a little too vertical for your taste. Your gentle lisp. Your hands, the safest I've ever known.

Melissa Febos writes, *Sometimes you love someone most of all when you are leaving them.*

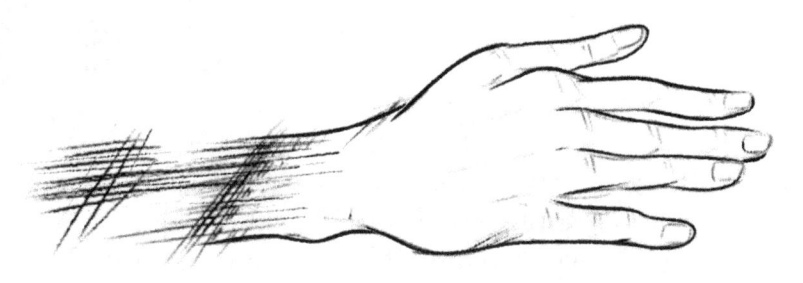

At one in the morning, lying beside you in your bed, I tell you you're hard to read. I tell you it's humiliating to always be the one who wants the other person more. I tell you it's hard to live in the present when you've told me from the start it's going to end someday. You tell me I'm projecting – according to you, everyone else thinks you're easy to read, so this must be a me problem. You tell me it's not useful to think of love quantitatively. You tell me I let myself be consumed by my emotions while you're just more pragmatic.

The processing takes so long, goes so deep, that it becomes an aphrodisiac. You go down on me in the dark. I fuck you from below. After you fall asleep, I roll on my side and let shame swallow me. You told me we had an expiration date. I knew this and I loved you anyway and that makes my desire my own fault. Why do I always have to want so much? Worse, why do I always have to admit it?

I let your rip current drag me into open ocean, dark uncharted waters swallowing me whole. It seems impossible that someday I'll choose to swim back to shore. It'll take me longer than I think. But nearly one year on, I'll find my way back to my friends. I'll find my way back to my family. I'll find my way back to writing. I'll feel the itch of anniversary before I understand what it is. I'll take my laptop out to the back porch of a sage-green house in Hudson, saturated in early spring sunlight, and the words will start pouring out onto the screen, and with them, I will finally feel the pieces of myself start to come back together.

It's a bleak March morning, grey and heavy. I am standing in my kitchen making coffee. We are on the brink. In five days, you will come to my apartment and end things for good. You will say a laundry list of hurtful things that you don't even seem to realize are hurtful. You will say, *I don't know why we both knew this wasn't going to last.* I will want to scream that you never let me forget it. I will want to remind you that this was always your choice, not mine.

Instead, I say nothing. Instead, I let you give me enthusiastic, patronizing suggestions for how to get over you: *You know what might help? Get a tattoo. Cut your hair maybe? Or get a piercing!*

On my way over here, you say, *I didn't even know how this conversation was going to go. But once I saw you, I knew.*

Why are you smiling so much? Does it really feel that wonderful to lose me?

I would have done anything to make it work, I sob into my hands.

You wrap an arm around my shoulders. I want to pummel you,

force you to feel even an ounce of all the weight you have made me carry.

Instead, I lean my head on your shoulder. Instead, I breathe you in.

I know, you say, and I feel sick to my stomach. This is the most pathetic you have ever made me feel. Somehow, still, I feel a pang of empathy for you, for the horrified reactions that the recounting of this moment will elicit for the rest of my life.

The playlist I never gave you is playing in the background. "Not Strong Enough" leaks from my laptop speakers. You laugh. *This is good timing for the new boygenius album, huh? Or maybe bad timing.*

You say, *I think love can be meaningful even if it's fleeting.* I look at you. It feels like I am seeing you for the first time, and who you are is a person that drops the L-word as you're breaking up with someone. Haven't you played with my devotion enough?

I force my voice into firmness. I deserve one cruel moment of my own. *Who said anything about love?*

I said I think that you're special, you told me once that I'm selfish, and I kissed you hard – and back again, around and around, that was how I loved you. My heart spins and my head throbs and my friends, where are my friends, where is everyone? Or am I the one who's lost? Three and a half months and my Word documents and my chest are still empty, aching. How much of this was my own doing? At the end, you said that you *didn't want me holding on for something that's never going to change*. Like most things you said to me, it stung, but this time because you were right – if nothing else, you'd always been honest. We both knew I was always going to fight for us. We both knew it would have to be you who set me free. Leaving me was the kindest way you ever broke my heart.

After the fracture is mostly complete, we sit on a bench in Washington Square Park to exchange books. I study the tiny sunbursts of daffodils blooming across from us. The sky is soft spring blue, puffs of cotton clouds dotting the expanse. I feel myself coming back to life with the world. You try everything to keep me from leaving, even though you're leaving me. You insist we stay friends. You ask me not to unfollow you on Twitter. You invite me to come with you to a Paramore concert in two months. You say our connection is special and you don't want to lose it.

I've never done this before – I've never cut anyone off, you say sadly. *I don't know how. I'm not like you.*

I know better now. I know you're really just afraid of losing access to someone you've trained so well. I let your subtle barbs slide off my skin. I keep my convictions firm. I keep my sunglasses on. You don't get to have my transparency anymore.

I have to do this, I tell you. *I just have to do this for me.*

YOU SAID EVERY TIME YOU HIT YOUR VAPE YOU THINK OF ME

and how I told you it was going to kill you someday. It never made sense to me that someone who literally hikes (and bikes, and surfs, and runs, and a million other healthy habits I could never maintain) would intentionally nuke their lungs, and in such a juvenile way to boot. For decades we've known how deadly nicotine is. We've known about vantablack lungs, about mutilated nucleotides. We could've been the generation to end smoking, but instead you sat on the mattress with your arctic blue vape pen strangled in your grip, thin white vapor clouding from your lips.

We were hovering in the heady, crackling static before the kiss that would lead to us making love for the last time. Hours before, over the phone, we both decided it would be the last time, which lent a pleasant lightness to the whole thing. When there's nothing after, there's no use trying to fix anything. You can just have fun. And we had fun, even while you blew a stream of smoke away from me and I told you it was disgusting. You just laughed and said you knew.

Thirteen years before I was born, my grandmother's lungs choked her to death from the inside out. She never had time to conceive of me, never met the woman who would grow me, never imagined there'd be a little girl someday who possessed her same fury, her same humor, her same vibrancy, staring at her photos and never once praying to God – always to her. You do not need to care about this. I say this to protect myself. You've already shown me you won't. I don't know why I have a vested interest in the continued rise and fall of your chest. You offer me less than she ever has. At least she brought me to life. You pushed me the closest I've been to the edge of it in years.

Sorry. I promised I wouldn't do this. It's hypocritical anyway. I know all about addictions. I'm here, aren't I?

THE CONSEQUENCES OF TRUTH

On March 13, 2020, as the veil wore thin and the world became ghostly and a new, deadly virus ripped through the planet, New Zealand dreampop band Yumi Zouma released their third studio album, Truth or Consequences. *On March 13, 2020, I was in San Francisco for spring break of my junior year of college, frantically refreshing my email to see if our university president had decided whether we'd all be evicted and whether I'd have time to go back to campus and rescue all my earthly possessions from my dorm room. I was also barely holding on after a cataclysmic heartbreak. As I sequestered in my father's house in upstate New York during the months that followed, this record became one of my only tethers to reality. What follows is my honest, very gay reaction to* Truth or Consequences *during one of the most deranged periods of my life, track by track. You're welcome.*

(Initially, this piece was co-written with the writer Uma Dwivedi when we were both in undergrad. We split the album down the middle – I took five, and they took five. The original essay has been lost to time – the online magazine we wrote it for has gone defunct. For this version, I've written my own interpretations of the tracks Uma initially covered: "Southwark," "Sage," "Mirror To The Fire," "Truer Than Ever," and "Magazine Bay." Yumi Zouma forever.)

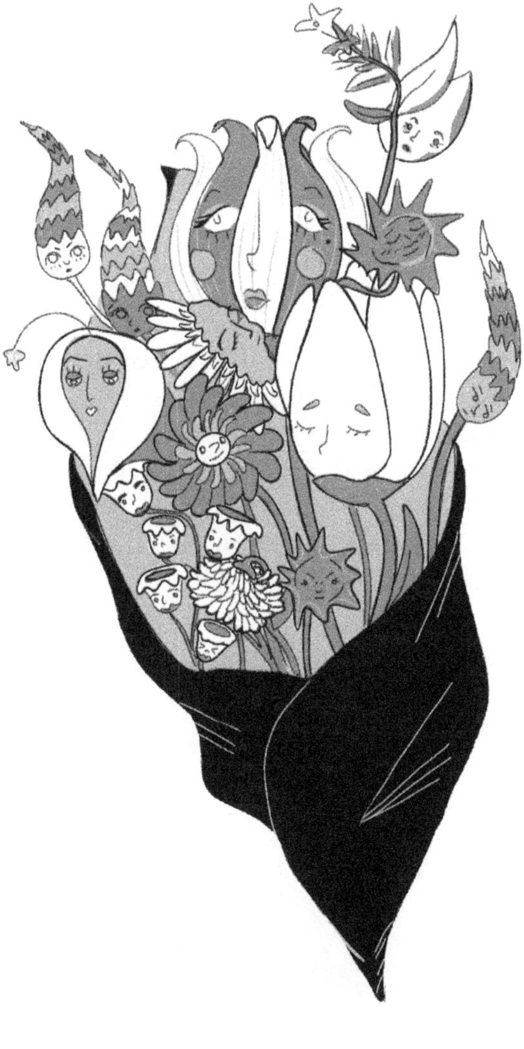

LONELY AFTER

Hi there. It's me again. I ran here for you, do you know that? I ran every one of those hundred miles. I rode every bus and plane and train just to feel your hands on my skin. Hi there. It's me again, and I'm overflowing into you. Sorry you're drowning, but I can't help it. You have to drink my feeling down until it makes you sick or we're both going to suffocate. It's embarrassing, but I've told myself I don't care so many times I can almost believe it. It almost doesn't sting when you ignore my messages and leave me hanging over the edge to save yourself. Listen to this song when you're hating yourself for waiting for me to come back, because no matter how cold you try to be, you know I always will.

RIGHT TRACK / WRONG MAN

We both got the choreography wrong. You spin into and away from me when you're not supposed to. I try to pull you back but you slip through my fingers. I'm choking on the cinnamon and smoke of you and my feet are moving in the wrong direction and I'm getting tired of this endless round and round. You make it easy to forget about you, because every single time I think we're getting the hang of this, you see *her*. You meet her eyes in the crowd and you can't remember how you melted for me when you could finally put your softness somewhere that would only hold it, never asking for more than you could give. You can't remember what it was like to be devoured by such a violent desire for closeness that never allowed you to unfurl slowly into bloom. You can only remember her profile edged in sunlight through your camera lens and how her sheets felt against your skin, and you trip over my feet. I've told you a million times I'll let you go but you play this song, and you ask me for one last dance.

SOUTHWARK

I wish we had gone to the beach together, just once. The sun, the sand, all that blue. Both of us brown and dizzy in the heat. Kissing as the waves lap at our ankles. We have such bad timing. Our love is northeast autumn, fading gold, early dark. You can only hold me when we're in the aquarium of your bedroom and the windows are black. It doesn't matter to me. The world can fall away so long as I can still see your outline waiting for me in the long and crawling six-five-four PM shadows. I listen to this song and taste salt in the air and refuse my own complicity. I see it all skewed. Nobody's perfect, I've said it before, and I love you, and can't that be its own absolution? Can't you hear the crash of my heart? Can't you feel the seafoam spray of my want on your cheeks? I know you do. I know it burns.

SAGE

Your body wants what my skin can give you, but my heart is too alive, my words too full of expectation. I want it all. Mornings tangled in your satin sheets while your cat pushes random items off your dresser one by one, furious to not be the center of your attention. Interlocked fingers illuminated by the sun, for all eyes. What we have only exists in the blue. To imagine otherwise is to break my own heart. My friends tell me over and over that it shouldn't be this hard. I shouldn't have to curb myself. My stomach shouldn't twist every time I see your grey bubbles from two hundred miles away, constantly terrified you're about to deliver the final blow. I listen to this song to lower my blood pressure and remind myself what will happen if I beg.

MIRROR TO THE FIRE

I'm your open secret. I'm another body wearing your silk robe in the hall, tiptoeing beneath fluorescent stutter to the bathroom, performing self-consciousness. In reality I love being your hurricane. You invite it, you aren't stupid, you just turned into an adult so you're feeling extra bold off 3 PM cold brew and legal margaritas and you open your arms to the wind. Still, we don't discuss it, we hold the charge between us silently, we owe each other nothing. I'll see you a few hours after our private goodbye in the late morning light. You'll casually lean back in your chair with your legs crossed and toss a *hey* in my direction without meeting my eyes. On the subway to the bus station, I'll listen to this song and remind my heart it's not allowed to break.

COOL FOR A SECOND

God, I'm tired. Aren't you? Let's go back to that first night in your room before the territory was uncharted. Before you closed the door and I could still recognize myself as someone that hadn't loved you yet. Our fading feels like the end of the world. But we've both endured many small apocalypses in our lives. I can see it now. I can hold it in my hand. A spark that couldn't even catch the air to burn. It's okay. We'll still smile when the leaves start to change and we see each other on the sidewalk. You'll think about how all I could ever do was fall, and maybe you'll be grateful. I'll listen to this song and I'll cradle what you gave me and maybe, someday, I'll learn to let the embers be enough.

TRUER THAN EVER

Sometimes, I take time off from loving you. I work in the garden. I experiment in the kitchen. I make sourdough bread. I make candied lemon peels. I bare my body to the sun, unprotected, and pray for the fate of my grandfather. These days I am not so married to being alive. I feel guilty, sometimes, when I read the news and see the blood and feel nothing but envy. You cross my mind every hour. I knew all along we never stood a chance, but truth can't stop a beating heart. In a way, I'm relieved it's over, if only to staunch the pointless hope that gushed from my punctured arteries every time you held me in your arms. As another sleepless night turns to blue morning, I play this song to convince myself of the lie I can never believe: I'm better off alone.

MY PALMS ARE YOUR REFERENCE TO HOLD TO YOUR HEART

As it turns out, I wasn't built for this. I ignored my desire for softness so I could have you the only way you know how to be had: temporarily. We're in bed when you hit the bottom of my chin so hard my teeth snap together and rattle. I wasn't built for this. The soreness in my jaw says we have an understanding, but you still hold my hands to your heart the morning after and what the fuck am I supposed to do about that. If you had only been completely cruel instead of halfway. But I could tell you were surprised by me. I was more than you expected. Oh, who the hell do I think I am. This is not what it is. Nothing is. I throw myself onto my mattress in my pitch-dark room as this song blasts from my laptop and wish I could be stronger. I wish I could want love without risk.

MAGAZINE BAY

I have seen you once since the end. Walking by the store where you apparently work now, I catch a glimpse of your back through the wide front window, facing the cash registers and snake of customers, none of them understanding the gravity of their luck, the million to one chance that they're alive at the exact moment in time where they get to stand in front of you and look into your eyes. My knuckles reach for the glass that stands between my fingers and their former home at the nape of your neck. I can never forget what you've done to me, I can never forget the unmaking in the kitchen at nine in the morning or the tears on your cheeks or all your cruel words or the only time in my life when my voice shook along with my body as I told you to go fuck yourself. Still, I want to offer you tenderness. Still, I want to watch your anger melt away as you understand even a fraction of my grief. But as this song plays through my headphones, I know you have to tell yourself I'm the villain to make peace with your choices, to move on with your life. I let my hands fall away.

LIE LIKE YOU WANT ME BACK

Hi there. It's me again. Somehow I've made it this far without you, but if you change your mind I'll make it easy. No questions asked. No apologies necessary. I'm open. I promise. Hi there. It's me again. You didn't think I'd ever stop writing about you, did you? Hi. It's me. And as long as you're out there, it'll always be me. Again and again and again.

HARDLINE *After Julien Baker*

Wednesday morning and I decide to listen to your voicemail again for the first time in several weeks. While drinking coffee at my computer and waiting for a meeting to start, I find myself missing the way you said my name. I gave the pain permission earlier than usual today. Everything is so fragile. If I click the wrong button, I'll dial your number instead of the preserved starlight of your voice, the words dead and gone by the time they reach me. I've learned I need to be more careful. I click the button that lets you tell me again about the moon, huge and bleeding. You tell me again you're falling asleep on the road, so you pulled over. You tell me again you *just wanted to say hi*. My mind is a rural parking lot you keep trying to pull out of. Weeds shove their way forcefully through cracks in the asphalt. Teenagers smoke on the hoods of their cars, spin donuts, pop the exhaust like gunfire. An oil spill sunset drenches the sky in utter pinkness over the black flatline of trees on the horizon. I want to keep you here, revving your engine. Today I realized I was forgetting college and cried tears of joy. Does this mean someday the heartbreak of your freckled face on the pillow beside me, sweet and sleeping, will go the way of binge-drinking alone in seminar rooms after dark? It's hard to believe I was eighteen once. Dancing atop hardwood desks, writing the story of my loneliness on chalkboards beneath faded reading assignments, tilting my head back to pour a Poland Spring bottle filled with rum down my throat. I thought I could never be emptier. I hadn't met you yet. I thought I knew myself. I thought I knew what I needed and didn't. Every time your eyes meet mine I draw a hard line to save us both. Every time you touch me I cross it over and over. I can't stomach all this impossible want but I need to hear you say my name again. Rewind. Listen. Rewind. Listen. *Hi Mia. Hi Mia. Hi Mia. Hi—*

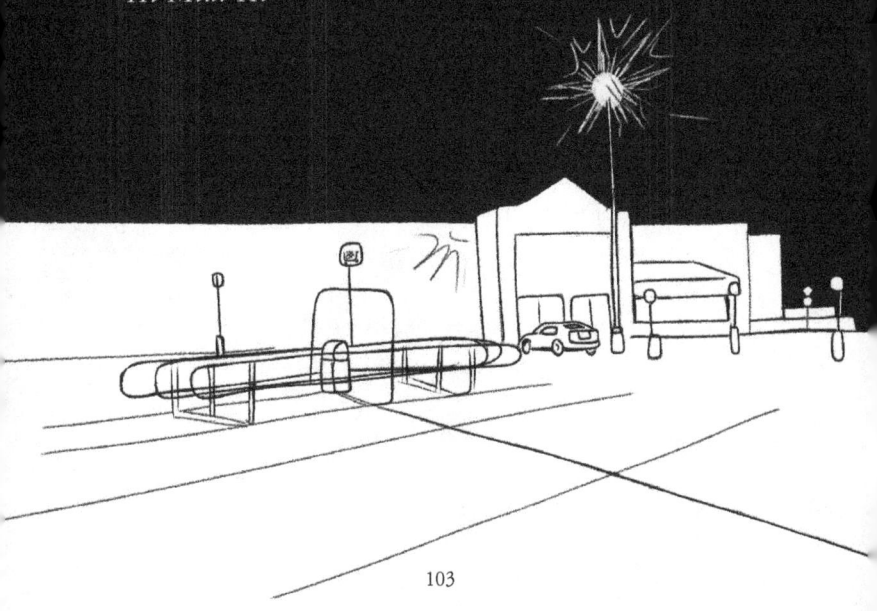

AOTY

MASSEDUCTION – St. Vincent

Spring break 2018. My dad and I are barreling up the California coast in a rental car we both wish was a convertible. I haven't been back here since my grandfather was buried eleven years ago. We've left my older sister behind in lush Los Angeles and are headed straight for San Francisco, the city that was supposed to be mine. Three months have passed since you sat me down in your dorm room and told me you *just didn't feel anything*. Not the way I did. I lower the window, smell salt. No one ever feels things the way I do.

My dad left me in charge of the music. I'm playing St. Vincent's latest album, recommended by the friend we share. As the months passed, the sadness crossed over into fury without my realizing it. Since then I've been trying to stay as angry as possible for as long as possible, because I never thought I'd ever make it out of the hurt. So far, St. Vincent is helping with that. Furiously pulsing synth, smooth, biting vocals, violent bass riffs.

I feel an unrelenting restlessness that in a couple years I'll come to recognize as mania. My dad's doing eighty on the open road but it isn't fast enough. The music strips down and I sink into the past. I've never shown the city that ended up being mine to anyone but you. I shut my eyes and your hair is blowing into your face on the High Line as you smile at my phone's camera. Your head is pressing against mine as we take selfies in the Glossier pop-up store. Your eyes are sparkling under the giant Christmas tree in Bryant Park, because it's still November so I can't give you Rockefeller Center. Barely breathing, I reach for your hand but stop just short of taking it. We both watch the ice skaters zoom around the rink and you whisper something I can't remember anymore, but I do remember the heat as I imagined you were saying it about me. *Incredible. Beautiful. Wow.* I wanted you to see that I could show you everything, if you let me.

I open my eyes and I turn to see the Pacific, bluer than anything has ever been.

About U – MUNA

Mid-Summer 2018. Every morning I wake up bruised. I thought I had gotten over it, I really did, but everything's sticky in the Connecticut summer and I have too much time to think. You're the only person who makes me feel sane. I go to your house every Friday after work. I walk. It's twenty minutes and I dance the whole way there with MUNA in my ears, slapping away mosquitos and imagining the euphoria of your air conditioning. We cook dinner in your tiny kitchen with the skylight over the sink. I unplug my earbuds and set my phone in a cup. You say it's a little too sad for you.

After the dishes are washed and the leftovers packed, that's when the danger starts. That's when you lie down on your couch and I burrow into your arms, and you rest your chin on the top of my head. You turn on the TV and we lay there, watching. Somehow, we can hold each other and not want the same things. You want things to stay how they are. I want more. I always want more.

So I try dating boys for the first time in my life. There's one in particular who will keep coming back for years, long after I finally understand my indifference. In spite of his girlfriend he'll call me in the middle of the night because he saw me on the street all velvet and glow and he *just wants to know what I'm up to,* and of course I'll say no, but he'll hear my smile because I like the idea of having enough power to take things from people. I'll like this idea even more a year from now. But I don't know it yet. I just know that the people I want have two things in common: they're not men, and they don't want me. So I beg my body to feel what it can't, and when it can't, I punish it.

I walk home listening to "Around U" on repeat. The reverb in the opening seconds sounds like the name I've lost. Over and over again.

I find solace in gay synth and crying in public. I drink and don't eat. I waste days walking circles around campus and to the house twenty minutes away, earbuds in. The door always opens. At least we both know we're using each other.

Bury Me At Makeout Creek – Mitski

Late Spring 2019. I wasn't even supposed to be at this party, but my friends are still full of energy and want to make the most of the night. They dragged me down the street promising a good time, promising you. I can talk myself into anything, including that you love me, too. So I decide to be a good friend. I walk behind them on the sidewalk. When we get to the house I peer through a hole in the fence and I see you kissing him. There's fairy lights in the backyard. He holds your hand, I think. It's nice.

This one lasts far longer than seems possible, given how little I will remember of it later. I am hormonally imbalanced, freshly violated, prone to melodrama. Everything is devastating and euphoric. You are there and beautiful. You write poems about Mitski that are really about the men you choose. I am always right about them, but you just think I'm a lesbian. I start listening to the same stripped electric guitar, every chord holding the rage and anguish of women like us, always waiting to be chosen back. This is when I start conflating revolution and the taste of salt on someone's skin. This is also when I learn that the only person stopping me from filling my water bottle with rum is myself.

While I'm walking you home from a party one night, you stumble on three margaritas, two Moscow mules, and a tequila shot. I hold you up and you say you love me. You say it makes you sad that I never say it back.

On the other side of the fence my friends are saying he means nothing, you're different around me, you don't know what you want and I laugh in their faces. You want me, and you want normalcy, and you know you can only have one. In five months I'll sit on my bed and you'll sit at my desk and you'll tell me you think you're *too trapped in compulsory heterosexuality to be with a woman*. You don't know how lucky we are that I already spent April mourning you. You're the only one I never tell.

Willowbank – Yumi Zouma

Summer, Fall, Winter 2019. (And again, Summer, Fall, Winter 2021. It will be identical. I don't know this yet.) You're my first. No qualifiers, no *almost sort of kind of maybe not this time.* No, you *are*. First to grab my messy bun and squeeze it in tender playfulness before I go down on you. First to look up at me through your eyelashes. First to be surprised by me. I can see it in the way your thigh bounces as you light a cigarette before we fuck. You don't know how good I am at noticing things. You don't stay long enough to find out.

You are so separate from a suffocating life I've been trying so hard to escape. An entirely different city, an entirely different set of rules. I know who you belong to, and it's never me. Yet I am the one chosen to bear witness to your body shimmying beneath the harsh fluorescent light in the CVS, beat for beat with the Yumi Zouma song crackling through the intercom.

In the millisecond before the meteor hits, I make a new list. I justify: I love people who dance in public and don't give a damn what others think about it. I love people who wear necklaces and smell like smoke and read and write. I love people who absorb me. I love people who turn me into someone free and feral who will do anything for one more taste. Someone unafraid. But now everyone is afraid of me. Everyone who isn't you becomes collateral. For the first time I don't care what it will cost. I commit to break my world and soul for you. I step off the cliff and stand upright on air.

We stretch out before ourselves. What we do, what two mistimed people have always done, only ever has one ending. It will never be clearer than it is right now. I grin so wide you can feel it from a yard away and you look at me and laugh. My eyes say *Give me everything you've got. I'm ready. I've been waiting for you all my life.*

You do. It burns. I barely make it out alive. You don't know how to apologize. You stand above and watch as the edges dissolve around me. I fade to black with a heart bursting with all the love you wouldn't take and I know I'll forgive you anything.

Miss Anthropocene – Grimes

Winter 2020. *Wake up. Get up. Claw your way back to consciousness. Get up. Get the fuck up. Look at the ruin you've made of your life. Stare it in the eyes and don't you dare look away.*

I've done it now. Wine bottles cover the floor. I can't blame you for not wanting me, but I can blame you for everything else. And I do.

Last night while the belt was still coiled around my neck I was thinking *I know it should not hurt as much as it does,* I was thinking *I have always been so disproportionate,* I was thinking *This was just a rebound anyway* but to be frank after Yumi Zouma in the CVS I was already barely holding it together. I still have your confession stored as a grey text bubble of ones and zeroes. To admit to someone that you broke them intentionally, that you saw their affection and recognized it for what it was, used it to stroke your own ego until it became more human than fun, takes a degree of cruelty I cannot understand and a degree of bravery I cannot help but respect.

I think I might be an addict. Drugs, drinking,

women who apparently plan ahead to discard me. I lie on my twin XL mattress blasting "You'll miss me when you're not around" and wonder, just like I did last night, if the rest of my life is worth living if someone can treat me this way. Grimes seems to agree. Her new music is dark and apathetic, a soundtrack to giving in. There was a time when I idolized her, when her music saved me from myself. So when she tells me that she'll drown herself by tying rocks to her feet and she'll smile at the bottom of the river, it feels personal.

But somehow, even in this pathetic aftermath of hope, there's still something stubborn in me, something scolding. It's not *fight* or *strength* or any of the words they use to imply you're worth less for wanting to die. It's an illusion that stings enough to make me scream to life, to stick me full of spiteful survival: *there's more.* I open my eyes. I stand.

Present Tense – Yumi Zouma

Winter 2022.

I leave the city, saturated with grief. I go home to where the nights are silent and the roads are choked with trees. There's space to think here. What has left me floats in the air around my head. I imagine I could reach out and touch them, if I wanted. Complicated women, losing me.

In your eyes, I was *passionate*. I was *hardworking*. I *inspired you*. You gave me a note before the end. I keep it beside my laptop. I carry it in my pocket when I leave the house. You wanted me so much you came back after two years. You wanted me too much, so you gave me up. It doesn't change the fact that you saw me. You gave me back to myself. I wish I could thank you for that.

Yumi Zouma returns in parallel. Possibility is the order of the year. I have never needed anything like I need the unrelenting optimism of their new lyrics and the joy of their saxophone solos. I listen to "In The Eyes Of Our Love" and I ache in mourning. I listen to "Give It Hell" and I harden with hope. I sleep late. I drink coffee. I dance to "Mona Lisa" and I survive. Regret is not a word I understand. I have never chosen wrong, because I've always chosen love. But now I'm starting over. I'm waking up and I am going to give it hell. I am going to shout and stretch and reach for everything that I'm going to make mine.

At night I walk outside and stand on the slow-rotting deck where I used to read as a child. January blisters. I can see the stars again, and I am not afraid.

PRELUDE TO A PROMISE
I KNEW I WOULD BREAK

Twenty-four now and I'm desperate again. Bought two Annie Ernaux books in the bowels of the Strand, drank pink wine at my desk and thought about faithlessness. Last week I told Olya when you lose hope in love, it's easy to lose hope in everything else. Nothing's so delicious as smoking in the kitchen. Let the hurt vaporize out the cracked window. Revel in the nauseating thrill of doing something that would make your mother cry. Missed my subway stop because I was listening to Julien Baker's *Turn Out The Lights* for the first time and was transfixed by the agony. Outside it's the kind of cold I used to *take* the way one does a punch or one more finger but now I'm twenty-four and I'm weak and peeled so the wind slices through me like the needle that would brand the ginkgo leaf I'm too scared to sit for into the flesh of my left shoulder. I saw a flash of your face tonight in a blonde wearing an oversized Rangers sweatshirt at the dyke poetry reading. I keep pushing back the deadline to let you go. This is a nothing poem. This is a choice and it only hurts me. We can both agree on so many things. Missed my subway stop again because I was listening to Julien Baker's *Little Oblivions* for the first time and she gave me permission to let my grief crush me. It was a relief to stop minimizing: this loss *did* hurt enough to immobilize. At the dyke poetry reading someone shouted *My girlfriend is locked in the bathroom!!!* Long before the firefighters with their axes, a poet kicked in the door and set her free. A Christmas metaphor. I wished you were there. A Christmas pipe dream. This was about me, at first. The *you* slithers in, always. I wish I knew if I meant for blame or credit. Every night I burn holes in my brain with a j trying for *Eternal Sunshine* and it's working too well but I don't care, I'll take it all back, one day all that will remain of you is what I choose to write down of this time in our lives and the rest I'll ash. I can already feel you fading – you were right. Everything does, eventually. I hope you finally learned to see portraits in the stars. I hope you don't teach them to her. There's a plane coming for me soon. It all could've been for you. *It's not that I think I'm good, I know that I'm evil,* but I tell myself I can make anything holy, even your celluloid sidewalks. When I dive into the new year closer than ever, choking on your smog and surf, the next person I open my legs for will be the sun.

ANATOMY OF BREAKUP SEX

Close your eyes. Here you are in her passenger seat again, vulnerable. She's an hour late to work but couldn't let you go just yet, so she asked if you wanted coffee. She knows you always want coffee. For the first time in years you left the house without makeup, or your wallet, or your phone. In pajamas and the same blue sweater you've been wearing for two weeks. Even slippers. You have never trusted anyone this deeply. It doesn't make sense. These things never do. It's eight in the morning. Lean back against the headrest. Feel the sun warm on your face through the car window and know you are safe. You ache to cry. Your body won't let you.

Remind yourself why. For release, for an end you could control. Really? Be honest. She's the one behind the wheel. Control is an illusion. You cannot break your emotions like a horse choking on the bit.

She lets you pick the music. You move on autopilot. Your body knows the song, the only song. She won't remember. She doesn't remember anything, not really. She's so sweet. This could never. You could never. You know this, but here you are. In the sun. Last night, driving you to the inevitable in the dark, she played "Loyal (EDD)" by Sudan Archives and pointed out the house she grew up in when you passed it and didn't mention her partner even once and you thought for the first time, *We are doing something bad.*

You did it anyway and you did it gladly. Giving what you wanted. Taking what you needed. You couldn't ask the hard questions, so you never had to hear the hard answers. It was easy. For you.

You're blessed to always remember the music. You can build an infinite playlist of your lovers. What's playing when you prepare to eviscerate yourself for them. What's playing when you prepare to leave them. *Loyal.* Don't laugh. Not in front of her, not now. Don't think of her partner's ghost, heavy on the whole of it. What a waste— DON'T think of it. Don't think of all the others. Don't think of all the shards you never had to see. By then you were long gone, exploding for someone else. Never look back. Keep burning.

Burning like the core of you as she pressed her tongue against all your breaking for the last time. Burning like the tears in your eyes as you held tight to the headboard with one hand and, with the other, brought her to the end of you – *you* as in *both* as in *two* as in *we* as in something that could've been but would never be *love.* Not the kind you need. Not the kind that stays.

You turn your head to the driver's side and crack an eye open. She's moving her fingers in time. Taps them on the wheel. Makes them dance. White light breaks across her knuckles. You will always remember this. Don't look up from her hands to the slope of her neck as she turns away from you to check for traffic. It will break you.

Did I not say enough? Did I say that I need your love? 'Cause I need your love.

It comes down to this. The sun — you're never on the open road this early in the morning. The light is the kind of bright that exposes. The light makes everything real. Her hands again, rough from saltwater, tanned from this same sun. It comes down to this. Her hands, reaching to turn off the lamp. Her hands, skimming above your hips, still close enough for you to feel the static *pull*. In the queen-sized bed that does not belong to you, in the bedroom that does not belong to you, in the achingly empty house that does not belong to you, in this falsely sunny city of freeways and plastic surgery that (thank god) does not and will never, ever belong to you, it felt like you were the only two people in the world, and it was awful.

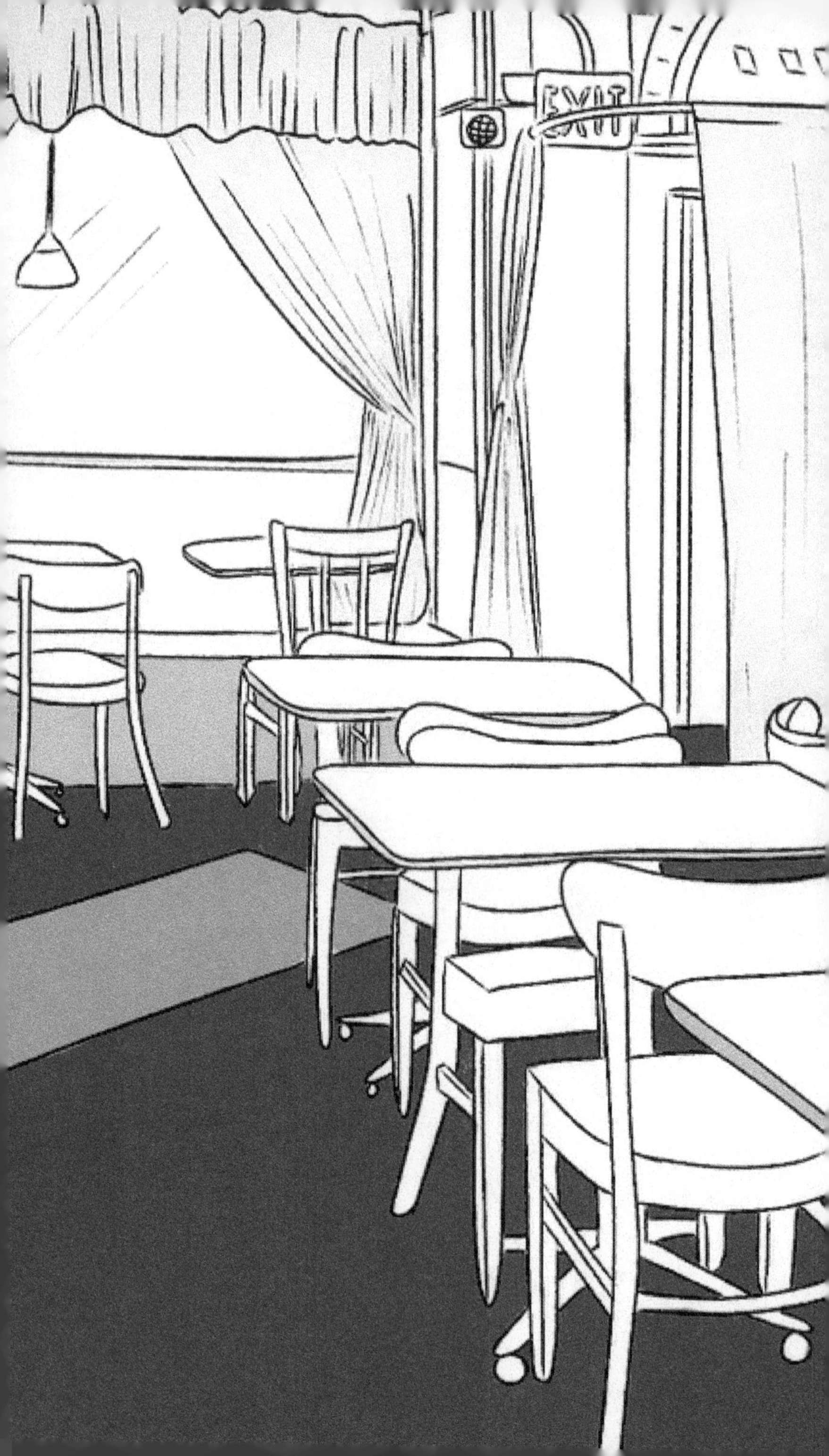
EXIT

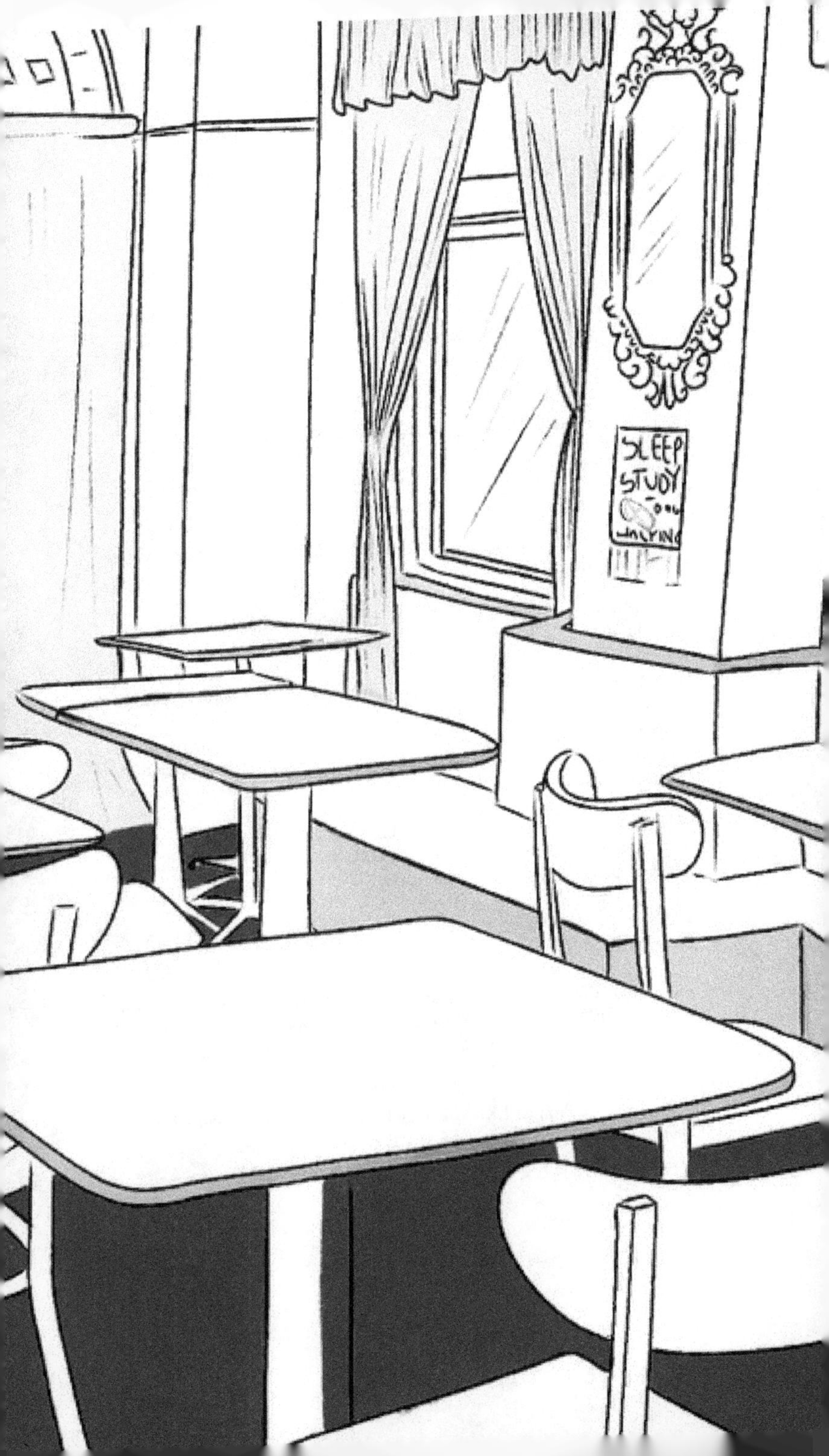
SLEEP
STUDY

ATTRIBUTIONS

Earlier versions of many fragments in this collection have been previously published elsewhere:

"Cambridge" was first published in Fifth Wheel Press's Flux Anthology in January 2022.

"i want to be on the golden state warriors dance team" was first published in Bullshit Lit's inaugural Bullshit Anthology in August 2022.

"The Woman Who Knows" was first published in Sage Cigarettes Magazine in November 2022.

"Crave" was first published in Copy in November 2023 and was inspired by the Paramore song of the same name.

"Hardline" was first published by VelvetPark Media in March 2024 and was inspired by the Julien Baker song of the same name.

"Letter To An Old Architect" was self-published in my newsletter, Overripe Peach, in March 2024 under the title "for the record." The new title pays homage to the boygenius song "Letter To An Old Poet." *I said I think that you're special, you told me once that I'm selfish, and I kissed you hard* are lyrics taken from the same song.

"Melatonin Dreams" and "Venice" were both self-published in zine format in April 2024 and sold to raise funds for eSIMS to be distributed among the Palestinian people trapped in the Gaza Strip.

"AOTY" was first published as a guest essay on Half Mystic Press under the title "There and Wanting."

"Anatomy of Breakup Sex" was first published in the zine ANATOMY OF BREAKUP SEX in February 2025 and features the lyrics *Did I not say enough? Did I say that I need your love? 'Cause I need your love* from the song "KPR" by Yumi Zouma.

In "Prelude To A Promise I Knew I Would Break," *It's not that I think I'm good, I know that I'm evil* is a lyric taken from "Even" by Julien Baker.

ACKNOWLEDGMENTS

Thank you to all early readers for your invaluable feedback: Polly Adams, Grace Caternolo, Ariana Matondo, and Emma Ratshin.

Thank you Rachel Ake Kuech for the gorgeous cover design.

Thank you Alex Alberto + Quilted Press.

Thank you Levi Wells for sharing your art. I've been wanting to do a project with you forever. Thanks for making our creative dreams come true.

Thank you Chloé Caldwell.

Thank you to my parents (who I hope didn't read this).

Thank you, Em. I am so lucky to be seen and loved by you.

Thank you, Peanut. :3

Thank you for reading.

—Mia

Thank you to my family and Fielding for your ceaseless care and support.

Thank you Atlanta.

Thank you service industry workers everywhere.

Thank you to my friends for loving me.

Thank you Mia for making me a part of this. All of your love and effort was worth it, it always is.

—Levi

ABOUT THE AUTHOR

Mia Arias Tsang is a writer and freelance editor based in New York City. Her work explores themes of queer desire, intimacy, and disconnect. A Tin House Summer Workshop alum, her work has appeared in *Autostraddle, Copy, Half Mystic Press, Fatal Flaw Magazine,* and *Broad Recognition Magazine,* among others. She is the program manager at the literary nonprofit House of SpeakEasy and writes a newsletter called "Overripe Peach." She lives in Queens with her cat, Peanut, and is currently working on a novel.

miatsang.com | IG: @mia.arias.tsang

ABOUT THE ILLUSTRATOR

Levi Wells is a trans multimedia artist and poet. His textile and illustrative works are devoted to real and unreal creatures, 2000's cartoons, and our changing human bodies. He lives in Atlanta, Georgia with his partner and two cats.

levi-levi.com | IG: @evil.vile.levi

ABOUT QUILTED PRESS

Quilted Press is a queer collective of independent authors. Our books reshape the traditional narratives of love, family, and identity—to offer new visions of ourselves and the future.

We founded Quilted Press to collectivize publishing and create a model that affords creative control and ownership to authors of non-traditional stories. Like the many pieces of a quilt, Quilted authors maintain their individuality while drawing from—and contributing to—the strength of the collective. Although every Quilted artist initiates and owns their project, the entire Quilted collective works together to bring each author's vision to fruition. Quilted Press practices writing as community. Together, we publish works that are as beautiful, powerful, and multifaceted as the individuals who create them.

quiltedpress.com | IG: @quiltedpress

www.ingramcontent.com/pod-product-compliance
Lightning Source LLC
Chambersburg PA
CBHW021456040225
21380CB00087B/698